S0-BDQ-802

A
Woman's
Own Golf Book

ALSO BY BARBARA PUETT
AND JIM APFELBAUM

Golf Etiquette

ALSO BY JIM APFELBAUM

Golf on $30 a Day (Or Less)

A
Woman's
Own Golf Book

SIMPLE LESSONS FOR
A LIFETIME OF GREAT GOLF

BARBARA PUETT

AND JIM APFELBAUM

ILLUSTRATIONS BY EDDY DAVIS

St. Martin's Griffin
New York

A WOMAN'S OWN GOLF BOOK. Copyright © 1999 by Barbara Puett and Jim Apfelbaum. All rights reserved. Printed in the United States of America. No part of this book may be used or reproduced in any manner whatsoever without written permission except in the case of brief quotations embodied in critical articles or reviews. For information, address St. Martin's Press, 175 Fifth Avenue, New York, N.Y. 10010.

www.stmartins.com

Library of Congress Cataloging-in-Publication Data

Puett, Barbara.
    A woman's own golf book / Barbara Puett and Jim Apfelbaum.
        p. cm.
    Includes index.
    ISBN 0-312-20393-4 (hc)
    ISBN 0-312-26415-1 (pbk)
    1. Golf for women Handbooks, manuals, etc. I. Apfelbaum, Jim.
II. Title.

GV966.P84 1999
796.352'082—dc21
                                              99-32244
                                                CIP

First St. Martin's Griffin Edition: May 2002

10 9 8 7 6 5 4 3 2 1

5/16/92

To: my good friend, pupil Barbara who I have watched hit many many good shots, few not so good but have enjoyed our association at all times. I hope this book will help you in, in your own teaching as well as your own game.

Fondly
Harvey Penick

Take dead aim and keep golfing with God and friends.

Harvey's inscription to Barbara in her copy of his "Little Red Book."

In the Mind's Eye

" 'No matter how I adjust, I keep hitting behind the ball,' Barbara Puett told me. She was too good a player to be doing this. 'Go out in your backyard. Keep swinging your 7-iron at a spot on the ground, a leaf or a piece of grass. When you can hit that spot regularly, come back and see me . . . if you need to.' There was nothing wrong with her swing. If she couldn't hit a spot, it was because her mind wasn't on it. Once she quit thinking about her swing and really put her mind into hitting a spot, the problem went away."

—HARVEY PENICK,
And If You Play Golf, You're My Friend

Contents

Introduction

This book is written for women who do other things than play golf. My professional life has revolved around the game, but I've also led an active life outside of golf as a wife, mother, school-teacher, and businesswoman. I've served on boards, been active with charities, and worked to improve my children's schools—experiencing the same stresses, battles, and joys familiar to working women and housewives. These points of reference have helped me better relate to my students in teaching the game to educated, busy, successful people, enriching my life in the process.

The only golf instructor I ever had was Harvey Penick. He taught me how to play. His legacy to me as a mentor was a teaching philosophy emphasizing simplicity, respect for the individual, and a lively, self-deprecating sense of humor.

In all the years I took lessons from Harvey, I never knew I ever did anything wrong in the golf swing. Two academically gifted daughters and a son with learning disabilities also taught me the importance of accentuating the positive and appreciating each individual's talents.

I've also been fortunate to enjoy close friendships with two of the all-time great professional golfers, Tom Kite and Ben Crenshaw. Reminiscing about Harvey with them has served to reaffirm his methods and the soundness of the fundamentals.

To that add a lot of sweat equity. Many thousands of students have provided me with an outstanding ongoing teaching laboratory. My students have made me a better teacher, and you have, in this book, the benefit of years of refinement.

Why is this book different? It doesn't draw a gender line in the sand. It doesn't take too much for granted. This is a book for those who may not follow the pro tours, read the magazines, or talk the talk and walk the walk. It doesn't talk down to the reader and it doesn't assume too much. The real-world examples have been tested over time. I know they'll help you enjoy golf to the best of your ability.

Note to Southpaws:
In the interests of brevity and clarity, this book makes an unfortunate concession. The instruction is presented for those of the right-handed persuasion. Where you see "right" read "left" and where you read "left" read "right." By holding the illustrations up to the mirror, the instruction will magically look more familiar.

A
Woman's
Own Golf Book

CHAPTER
1

Putting:
Painting the Way to the Hole

I'd like to learn to play golf.
I want to lower my scores.
I want to play in a tournament.

My teacher, Harvey Penick, made sure every one of his students appreciated the importance of putting and never lost sight of its value.

Harvey believed the putting green was the best place to begin learning golf. After all, we use the putter more often than any other club. The most difficult part of the game for the professional player, putting is the easiest introduction to golf for the beginner. While the tournament player must sink putts to win, the newcomer need only learn distance control.

Putting's importance to playing well can't be overstated. Every hole and every round ends with a putt. Putting begins building continuity in one's game, laying the foundation for chipping, pitching, and the full swing. Competitive golfers will be the first to tell you that the green is inevitably where tournaments are won and lost. Professional golfers rely upon their ability to putt consistently, and often spectacularly. Those who don't soon find other ways to make a living.

Sinking a putt is an undeniable pleasure. We receive positive feedback, reinforcement, and confidence. Newcomers making a first attempt share the satisfaction of the seasoned pro. They can also share something else: proper technique. Just how much they have in common reminds me of one particular student.

I had a group of professional women on the practice green one morning. Many had never before held a putter in their hands, let alone played any golf. My next lesson was a private one with Teresa, a better player who was having putting problems. She arrived early and watched the class go through its paces on the putting fundamentals of grip and stance, ball position and stroke. When the class ended and Teresa began her lesson, she couldn't miss.

"Why did you want this lesson?" I felt compelled to ask her.

"After watching the class," she said, "I realized what I needed to do."

It was a minor adjustment. Teresa noticed it and cured herself, another lesson in the enduring value and simplicity of the fundamentals. **For newcomers and experts alike, the basics never change.** As often happens, she just needed a refresher. She got it watching the beginners. I lost a lesson but the better my students play the happier I am.

There's a wonderful irony about putting, a game within the larger game of golf. While it may be the easiest aspect of golf to learn, putting beguiles the experts. For something so straightforward, it offers a sterling test of nerve and judgment. The game's long and distinguished history is positively littered with tales of heroism and tragedy that turned on a putt. The legendary Bobby

Jones once recalled that standing over one of only a few inches he felt himself "quivering in every muscle." Putting will never become ordinary and it can never be taken for granted.

Elusive as it can be, the best golfers have always been terrific putters, rehearsing with the diligence of top musicians practicing their scales. The fact remains: No matter how well we're driving the ball or hitting our irons, the buck stops on the green. A missed six-inch putt counts the same on the scorecard as a 200-yard drive—one stroke, no more, no less.

For something so important, putting requires no more strength or dexterity than wielding a paintbrush. It's often characterized as more of an art than a science, a part of the game that allows for and even encourages a certain creative, artistic expression, eccentricity, and even genius. Perhaps that's why putting's often buried or glossed over in instruction books. Within the framework of the fundamentals, putting individuality, no matter how offbeat, is permitted—assuming, of course, that it works.

Before going any further, let's acknowledge a genetic blind spot in golfers. Everyone wants to hit the long shots. They're fun to practice, much more dramatic than stroking little putts. There's always room on the practice green, while the driving range is often crowded. The range seems to emit a magnetic pull and the hypnotic effect of hitting one ball after another quickly draws us in. Every golfer wants to savor the sensation of hitting it long every time out. That's human nature. But golf is more than a game of distance. It's a game of accuracy. And, as an Irish caddie once wryly noted, "the little ones count as much as the big ones." Those who can pull themselves out of the seductive orbit of the driving range will find that regularly spending even a few minutes on the practice green pays dividends.

This sounds like the beginning of a bad golf joke but it's a true story. There was a golfer, it happened to be at a club in Cleveland, who had the misfortune to break his back. Golf was out of the question for a year, doctor's orders. While Frank couldn't play, or do much of anything, his wife insisted he get out of the house and spend time at the club. Since he was there anyway, Frank figured he might as well be productive. He could barely move around, let alone take a full swing, but he found he could putt and hit short chips without discomfort. These he did conscientiously during the months of recovery. When he could finally play golf again, Frank was astonished by the fantastic scores he was shooting. He even won his club championship, a title which he had always desired but realistically knew he never stood much chance of winning. Studious practice turned him into the club's best putter. Yes, there is a moral, if not a punchline. One needn't suffer a broken vertebrae to see the value of practicing the shots around the green. Practicing putting and the entire "short game" (as the shots hit from about one hundred yards and closer to the green are known) may not have the sizzle of banging balls, but it's time well spent.

Your mother should know   **PUTTING STANCE**

You'll think your mother is with us at various times throughout the book. Discussing the golf stance is one of them. Of course, mother only wanted what was best for us. With respect to good posture, she had it exactly right.

When she told us to hold our heads up and keep our backs straight, she wanted our appearances to be proud. Proper posture is routinely seen as preventing a slew of ailments, among them swayback and pinched nerves. Good posture makes us feel good and look confident. Poor posture makes us look and feel tired, so much so that a beauty expert calls it "the most common crime against the body." Just as mothers rightly view it as an important component to an attractive and healthy appearance, good posture remains a cornerstone of good golf.

Everything I Learned About Golf I Learned in Kindergarten is an unlikely title, but let's turn back the clock for a moment. Remember leaning over and swinging the elephant's trunk? That's the ideal golf stance. The back straight with the arms hanging naturally allows freedom of movement. When the arms hang naturally the hands hang beneath the shoulders, where we hold the putter. Some golfers prefer the arms to hang straight down to grip the putter. Others may bend their arms slightly. The idea is to get the rear end out of the way so the arms can swing freely *à la* an elephant's trunk. With the head up, bend from the hips and flex the knees slightly. **With good posture, we won't have to make later compensations or adjustments in the putting stroke or the golf swing.** Years of poor posture, of forcing the body into unnatural and uncomfortable positions, results in self-induced back pain for many golfers, particularly in the lower back. It brings us full circle to a mother's common sense. Beginning the game with good posture is sound, preventive maintenance.

Pleased to meet you   PUTTING GRIP

Gripping the putter couldn't be easier. Ninety-five percent of newcomers correctly hold it without instruction. Nevertheless, since putting inspires a lot of improvisation and originality, grips can get interesting, even bizarre. Golfers are always experimenting, searching for the magic. Every now and again, a tour player will even go so far as to putt one-handed.

Harvey introduced the grip this way: he'd face the student,

This is a popular putting grip. The thumbs point straight down the shaft.

extend the putter grip, and ask that she shake hands with the club, first with her left hand, then with her right. The grip is no more complicated than that. **Shake hands with your putter; after all, you hope to become good friends.**

Putter grips are flat along the top so it's pretty clear where the thumbs go. Some players hold it with all ten fingers on the grip. Others overlap the left index finger over the fingers of the right hand. Some prefer to have their left hand on top, others their right. Any of these methods is acceptable providing it feels good.

Squeeze play

Grip pressure is a concern with all the clubs, especially the putter. **Nothing will ruin a putting stroke or a swing more effectively than tension.** Let the air out of the balloon. Relax. **Hold the putter as you would a dinner fork:** lightly. For a surer feeling of control place it more in the palms than in the fingers, still holding it gently. Placing the putter more in the palms reduces twisting, or "breaking" the wrists during the stroke, a fatal flaw. With a good stance and a confident grip, it's time to step up to the ball.

Where should the ball be?   **BALL POSITION**

You'll find it easier to have the ball a couple of inches left of center, closer to the left foot than to the right.

On every shot you make . . .

The overwhelming desire to do *something* to the ball routinely causes tension in the upper body, especially when preparing to putt. **Get in the habit of consciously relaxing the elbows and shoulders. This will be a maxim repeated on every golf shot.** Professionals routinely use conscious breathing exercises and relaxation reminders like shaking out their hands or adjusting their clothes to help them recognize and deflect stress. The stakes may not be the same but all golfers experience pressure.

The truth and nothing but   **PUTTING STROKE**

The most fundamental truth about putting is that the hands must stay even with or be in front of the putterhead as it strikes the ball. A quick story. Before Ben Crenshaw left Austin to play in the Masters several years ago he visited with Harvey,

Notice the hands are over the ball, which is a little left of center. This gives them a head-start.

as it turned out for the last time. Harvey's final lesson for Ben, considered among the game's best putters, was a putting lesson. The tip he gave Ben was so basic—and so sound—that it helped him win the famous tournament and conquer Augusta National's notoriously fast greens. The reminder was simply for Ben not to let the putterhead get ahead of his hands in making the stroke.

What *exactly* does this mean?

Grip the club. Now take your stance and move the hands a little left (in the direction you're going), ahead of your zipper or navel. **The hands should be over the ball looking down.** This offers a slight head start.

Imagine a broom and a dustpan. To sweep dirt into the pan the broom handle tilts a little forward. Your arms and hands pull the broom through the dust sweeping it into the pan. Should the bristles get ahead of the hands, they'll point at the dirt and some of it will be left behind. Stop the hands at the dirt, let the broom-head go, and dirt flies all over the place.

It follows, then, that the most effective technique for achieving optimum broom mechanics—and a sound putting stroke—is to take a nice, smooth sweep with the hands leading the way. Sweep the ball into the hole.

Leading with the hands is essential to good putting. The sooner the newcomer can repeat it and the longer the advanced player can maintain it, the more success each will have. That a putter of Ben Crenshaw's caliber needed a reminder on something so elementary just shows how elusive putting can be. It also serves to remind us of the power of the fundamentals. If thinking about a broom strikes you as too much like housework, let's try some other, more pleasant, analogies.

Sweep the ball,
or paint a nice
stripe straight
to the hole.

The paint follows the brush

On a short putt imagine painting a nice even stripe to the hole. The putting stroke, like a brushstroke, should be smooth and low. The thought of painting a stripe to the hole keeps the putter on track through the ball. Or imagine brushing crumbs off a table. The hand leads and sweeps the crumbs the same way a putter leads and sweeps a ball.

Visual imagery, analogies, and metaphors are endemic in golf. They help us transfer our understanding of something we know how to do and now do without thinking—driving, sweeping, riding a bike, etc.—to something as yet new and unfamiliar (in this case, putting). As difficult as it is to learn a skill for the first time, once we get it right, it becomes progressively easier, eventually becoming second nature. That's where we're headed. Establish and ingrain the feeling of the hands ahead of the putter through the stroke. Giving the hands a head start will not only help on the green, it will also help in getting the ball onto the green with chipping.

Painting stripes   **SHORT PUTTS**

A good place to feel the motion of painting a stripe or sweeping towards the cup is three feet from the hole, approximately the length of your putter. This is the distance we invariably face, perhaps more than any other, every time we play. Make it easy on yourself by picking out a hole on a flat section of the green. Practice painting that stripe so the ball rolls into the hole.

Taking it slow

One of the biggest tips to helping everyone's putting is to take the putter away slowly from the ball, and I mean *slowly*. I'm not suggesting downshifting for the entire stroke, only in taking the putter back away from the ball. Make a graceful exit.

You wouldn't carelessly back the car out of the garage with the dog loose.

That's the pace to begin putts: a slow brushstroke, **the pace we'd use in petting a cat,** the smooth, controlled stroke of a canoe paddle through still water.

Going back slowly makes it easier to know how far to come back and through. If you were throwing a ball to someone standing nearby, the arm would slowly come back. This provides accuracy, as it does in throwing a wadded up piece of paper into a wastebasket. The arm doesn't whip back. It winds up slowly.

We all have a tendency to make too fast a backswing. Surprise: the culprit is tension. Newcomers get anxious over a delicate shot and tournament players feel increasing stress as pressure intensifies. Withdrawing the putter slowly (as we do with all the clubs) gives our natural instincts a chance to kick in.

Long distance operator   **LONG PUTTS**

On longer putts, instead of painting a stripe, think of following one. Putt down the highway center lines. Travelling brings to mind speed, control, and distance. To putt well from long range, we'll need an awareness of all three. **Start the putter slowly back from the ball.** This allows us to feel how far we're going. Moving slowly gives us control, and a measure in the mind's eye of how far to bring the putter through.

The putting stroke never changes. It only takes two seconds: one for the backswing, one for the follow-through. It's the same with all golf shots. In putting, what varies is the length of the stroke. On short putts, we'll come back a few inches and go through a few inches. On longer putts, we'll increase our one-back-and-two-through. Like a metronome, **the backswing and the follow-through are always the same length.** Think of every putt as being the same, only longer or shorter. The only change is in the distance of the backswing and follow-through.

Taking the putter back slowly gives us time to feel the length of the backswing. Putts that go too far are often caused by quick backswings. Pressure of any kind causes a lack of control taking the putter back that leads to inconsistency. Putting with the correct speed is the key to controlling distance. When putts go too far, take your putter away slowly. Make your one-two shorter.

Taking aim

Line up putts this way: Take your grip and aim the putter at the hole. (If the putter has a dot or sight line on it, use that.) **Place the putter behind the ball and look at the hole as you move your feet into position.** Doing it this way guides the feet to where they need to be without having to think about their placement. This is what's meant by alignment, and it's critical.

It's not as easy as it sounds. The ball presents an unwavering distraction. You'll feel its mesmerizing urge. But once you've lined the putter up, focus on where you want the ball to go: The hole. Prolonged staring at the ball paralyzes the body. It percolates tension up from the hands to the wrists and into the elbows and shoulders. You can almost see the muscles tensing. The longer we're frozen over the ball, the more difficult a putt becomes.

When Harvey noticed a golfer staring at the ball, he'd ask if he remembered where the hole was. It's a captivating force, that ball, no question about it, but staring it down doesn't make sense. We *know* where the ball *is,* we need to focus on where we want it to *go.*

Once you've aimed your putter, hold it still. It's like lining up a picture on the wall before being certain enough to hammer in a nail. When you've got it exactly where you want it, trust that you've lined it up correctly. Concentrate on the hole, look down, and then stroke the ball. Listen for it to drop before looking up. Don't peek.

Pick out a spot and putt a straight line. The ball will curve to the hole. That's what is meant by playing the break.

Reading the "break"

What to do when the green slopes to the right? Subtle banks will cause a rolling ball to turn, or "break," one way or the other, sometimes markedly. Reading the topographical map of a green boils down to guesswork and experience. The more familiar the golf course, the more accustomed we become to its subtleties.

All putts are straight. No matter how much the undulation will affect a ball's roll, the putting stroke remains the same. Remind yourself to putt a straight line. It's not at all unusual to have a putt where the break necessitates lining up away from the cup, rather than at it. We'll sometimes wish the ball towards the hole, manipulating the putter with our stroke. In other words, we try to putt with a curved stroke. That's ineffective. **Have confidence every time by using the same basic stroke that only varies with length.**

Here's an excellent way of determining the break: Pretend you're emptying a bucket of water on the green between your ball and the hole. Which way would the water run? If you've read it correctly, that's the path the ball will take.

Breaking putts are tricky, deliberately designed to test our mettle and faith in our stroke. After deciding how the ball will react to the lay of the land, pick a spot, line up, and stick with it. Have confidence that you've made the right decision and putt the ball decisively to that spot.

To practice, pick a spot, a blade of grass, or a light spot on the green, to the side of the hole. Line up to it and putt a straight line. Hopefully, the ball will curve to the hole.

Wha' happen?

Check where your putter's facing when you've badly missed a putt. Is it pointed left or right of the hole, even just a fraction? Would your stripe be pointing somewhere other than to the hole? Is the putterhead even with your hands and arms? Remember the broom and the brush. When you miss sweeping the dirt into the dust pan, it's an easy adjustment to make; same with painting a crooked stripe. You can often correct flaws in your putting stroke by looking at the end of the stroke. It tells the unerring story of what came before.

Checking yourself in a mirror is a way of seeing what the

instructor sees. You'll be able to scrutinize your stroke and posture, and double-check that your hands are set ahead of the ball.

Checkpoints

This is what to do on the green to relieve tension, make your playing partners happy, and putt better than ever:

Take your grip and aim your putter at the hole.

Look at the hole as you put your feet in place.

Look at the hole as long as you like—relaxing as you look at it.

Look down at the ball for no longer than two seconds (three max).

Take the putter back slowly and sweep the ball into the hole.

Listen for the sound of the ball going in. (No peeking.)

Repeat this routine on every putt.

Expectations

After completing the above successfully and savoring the sound of the ball falling into the cup, I want to tell you what to expect on the putting green. Golfers are quick to criticize themselves when they miss putts. We can reasonably expect to hole the occasional putt from inside of ten feet, but keep in mind that the best golfers in the world only make fifty-five percent of their six-foot putts. A pitiful putt would be a six-footer that rolls by the cup, leaving a putt of that same length back. Be grateful for any putt over six feet that is close enough to be tapped into the hole

Practice will never make perfect, but the professionals still spend hours every week on their strokes. Televised golf tournaments often lead the rest of us to unfair expectations. The cameras follow the leaders, who seem to make a huge percentage of their putts. That's why they're leading the tournament. The same players may disappear from the screen the following week when their putting isn't "on."

You should feel confident about your ability to sink putts of three feet or less, but the pros miss these, too. Beyond three feet, the likelihood is a matter of chance. With good fundamentals and practice, your odds quantifiably improve. A little luck doesn't hurt either. The golf psychologists all seem to agree on this: If you don't think you'll make a putt, you probably won't. Keep an open mind and give the ball a chance to go in the hole. You may surprise yourself.

HOW TO PRACTICE

Compared to the entertainment value on the driving range, putting practice can seem like penance. It won't be so bad if you can make a game out of it. Start without a hole, putting three balls for short distances. Think about taking the putter back slowly, **going the same distance back and through.**

When you feel you've got the mechanics of the stroke down, move to a hole. Practice three-foot putts. Test yourself by making three in a row. If putts of this important length won't drop, there's no point in moving on. A three-footer is a litmus test of the stroke revealing much about our technique—whether the back swing is too fast, or if we've got the putter improperly aimed. On all your putts, listen for the ball to drop into the hole. Avoid the urge to look up too quickly. In other words, no peeking.

Harvey's favorite drill was simply to take one ball and putt it around the practice green. Going from one hole to the next practices the adjustments you'll make while you're playing. A longer putt doesn't tell us as much because we can't expect to make everything longer than three feet—but we should make our three-footers. Check at the end of the stroke that the putter is aimed at the hole.

Putting around the green, hole to hole, simulates the situations you'll face on the golf course where you'll never have the same putt twice. It's also easier on the back. Play nine holes around the practice green, keeping score if you like. Play nine holes in eighteen strokes and you're ready to move on to the course or practice tee. I watched Ben Crenshaw, one of the game's greatest putters, putt for hours this way around the Austin Country Club practice green as a boy.

Whatever you can do to make practice more fun and meaningful will be beneficial. Play nine holes with a friend or shoot for your personal best. Times passes quickly and games like these build confidence.

Chipping: Sweeping Pennies onto the Green

I want to begin learning the golf swing.
I need a sure-fire shot around the greens.
I really want to improve my scores.

It's a good rule of thumb to putt whenever feasible, even from off the green. It's commonly done from the green's edge, the area known as the fringe, collar, apron, or frog hair (and no, I have no idea where this last expression comes from). For any number of reasons, however, putting won't always be an option. The ground may be soft and wet, less conducive to rolling a ball, or the length of the shot simply makes it impractical. Another putting red flag is thick or patchy grass. **So putt if you can, chip when you can't.**

Short and compact, the chip is designed for accuracy, its hallmarks touch and control. With this shot we learn to hit the ball. Harvey likened it to a short drive because the chip contains the essence of the golf swing.

Good chipping can rescue less than stellar shots elsewhere on the golf course, a poor drive, or a wayward iron shot. When we leave them *stiff* (close to the hole in golf slang) chips take pressure off putting. To accomplished players, skillful work around the green is as much a part of their repertoire as an alfredo sauce is to a reputable Italian chef. It may not be the most dramatic shot you'll ever hit, but effective chipping builds confidence that carries over to the rest of your game.

Imagine a chipped ball as an airplane coming in for a smooth landing. The plane (ball) should land softly on the green and taxi up to the hole. A 7-, 8-, or 9-iron is the most popular club selection to chip, but the distance of the "runway" and the difficulty in getting the ball onto the putting surface are the deciding factors.

Getting a grip   CHIPPING GRIP

Like gripping the putter, how to hold a club to chip is largely a matter of personal preference. It's not until we swing for power that the grip becomes essential. Some golfers chip with the same grip they use to putt. Differences in height may determine where on the club a golfer places her hands. Some stand more erect and hold it on the end. Others prefer to bend over slightly and make the club shorter (more like the length of a putter), the thought being that doing so provides a better sense of control.

Along with the shoulders and elbows, consciously relax the hands. Hold the club as if it were a putter or a piece of silverware. Squeezing the club will not only develop blisters, it'll ruin any chance of a good shot.

Babe Didrikson Zaharias, arguably the best female athlete of the twentieth century and a fantastic golfer, took these notions to heart. She once confided to her good friend, Peggy Kirk Bell, that when she lifted a fork or knife, she'd delicately feel the weight and balance in her hands. "It helps my golf," she said.

At ease   **CHIPPING STANCE**

The chipping stance is similar to the putting stance, but with a longer club in our hands we'll stand more erect. Extend the rear end out slightly. Stand close to the ball (eight to ten inches from it), heels close together, toes slightly flared. This is referred to as an "open" stance. Many feel that it offers a better view of the hole. The upper arms stay close enough to touch the body. Here's how I remember it: When close to the green, stand close to the ball, feet close together, upper arms in close.

Line up to the hole as in putting, the feet remaining close together. Because we've got a club in our hands, there is a temptation to take a wider stance, to stand farther away from the ball—as if to hit a full golf shot. But, we're just a few feet off the green.

Weighty question

Lean slightly towards the green, that is, **in the direction you're going** (with weight more on the left foot).

Basic training

The most important chipping fundamental: **Keep the hands even with or ahead of the clubhead throughout the stroke.** Sound familiar? It's the same with putting, except in chipping, we're going to give the hands a little more of a head start. Move your hands toward the left thigh and position your feet so the ball is just to the right of center, a little closer to your right foot. This assures that the hands will maintain their lead during the shot. This shot is hit with a firm left wrist. I had great success in executing and teaching it when I had the misfortune of having broken my left wrist. Students the next day said they'd never understood chipping better than when seeing my wrist in a cast. Maybe I should've kept the cast.

If you'll think about sweeping the balls under an imaginary fence, you'll hit crisp chip shots.

Tips for chips

Chipping requires very little body movement. As with modern appliances, at least in theory, with fewer moving parts, there should be less opportunity for things to go wrong. Chipping is like threading a needle or returning an ice tray to the freezer without spilling. While one part of the body is involved, those that aren't stay still, most importantly the head. No wonder, then, that **keeping the head still is a tenet of a sound chipping stroke.** A steady head allows the club to swing through evenly and prevents erratic shots. The shot's accuracy comes from using the same slow back, low sweeping, one-two motion of a putt.

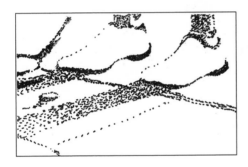

Got a penny?

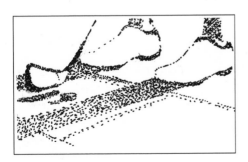

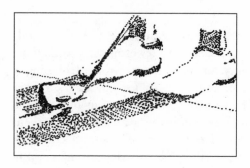

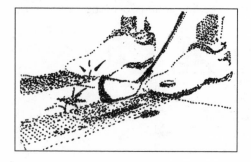

The only difference is that now, instead of a putter, we're using a club.

A penny for your chips

One reason why golf is so challenging is that often what we think will happen is just the opposite of what occurs. The game can sometimes seem to have a logic all its own, and these misconceptions can be a big deterrent to learning. Here's an example of what I mean: Deliberately trying to lift the ball in the air when we swing, we'll often top it instead. In fact, swinging low is what makes the ball go high. See what I mean? Here are some creative ways of coming to grips with this conundrum.

Got a penny? Place it a few feet off the practice green. The object here is to sweep that penny onto the green as if you were sweeping a mess into a dustpan. Now put a ball on top of that penny. Again, concentrate on sweeping that penny onto the green. It may not seem like much but this practice will help you hit all your shots crisply, chips included.

The ideal chip shot hops briefly and then rolls. Another way of thinking about the flight of a chip will appeal to those who garden. Let's pretend that several rocks have washed under the fence separating your yard from your neighbor's. You need to return those rocks. Sweep them back underneath the fence. Try and make the "rocks" go low. The result will be that your ball will jump like a dolphin before rolling—just like we want it to. Remember to try and make the ball go low, so it jumps into the air. Try and lift the ball into the air and it will roll uncontrollably along the ground. The trick is in believing that you are swinging through and sweeping.

This may defy logic, but that's the way it is. Know that when you lift up in the golf swing, the ball does the opposite.

Another way of thinking about chipping while on the golf course is to imagine a fence surrounding the green. The only way on is to sweep the ball under the fence. Sweeping keeps the swing short and compact. It brings the club straight through like a broom, and it helps you know instinctively how far back to take the club.

Step on it

Mrs. Lovejoy, a senior citizen and new golfer, was getting frustrated. Her chipping stroke was out of control. "I want you to accelerate only when you get to the ball," I said, emphasizing the key to good chipping. "That's why you have that nice, slow backswing, so you can accelerate on the other side coming through." It was a nice concept but it didn't click. Sweeping the penny didn't work either. And she wasn't a gardener. Finally, she turned to me and said, "Are you saying that I should step on the gas as I get to the ball?" Bingo.

Now I tell students to chip crisply by imagining their ball as a car stuck in an intersection. The light is changing. Beat the traffic by stepping on the gas at the ball.

There's no point in speeding up to enter the intersection, like Mrs. Lovejoy. But once we're in it, we need to hightail it—as we're striking the ball. Turns out that years earlier, my grandmotherly student had been a race car driver! It took awhile but she eventually understood the concept by relating it to her life experiences. Looking back, I think I got more from that lesson than she did. The image has helped countless others grasp the importance of accelerating the swing at the proper time.

It'll work for you, too. Just keep in mind an important distinction: **There's no rush to get the club back, or even to start it down, but once we get to the ball, step on it.** This will always give us a short, compact swing that we can control. For a short shot, a little acceleration. For a long shot, more acceleration as we chip it "under" the bench.

Taking aim

Wherever the club's aimed, that's where the ball's going—so aim the clubface carefully. **As in putting, make certain the bottom line of the iron (the leading edge) is pointed towards the hole.** After you've aimed it, hold the club steady. For perfect

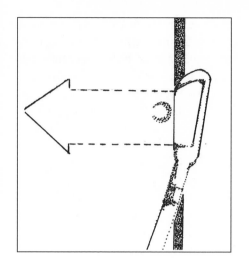

This is how you'll aim every golf club. The leading edge (bottom line) faces your target.

alignment, focus on the target while moving your feet into position.

Look at the hole as long as you like, relaxing the arms and shoulders, but peer down at the ball no longer than two or three seconds. Then, look at the ball and sweep the grass as if there were a penny underneath the ball. One begins the stroke, two finishes it. Like the playground swing, there's no pause in the middle. Should the ball go left of the target, check the club position after the swing. Is the clubface turned left? Just like the putting stroke, the chip goes straight back and straight through. Line up carefully before the shot. We can't make compensations for poor aim.

Which club to use?   CLUB SELECTION
The bottom line in chipping is: Pick the club that will get your ball onto the green and rolling as quickly as possible.

Any club can be used, but the important thing to remember is that the swing doesn't change. Suppose your ball lies a couple of feet off the green in thick grass and the hole is less than ten feet away. This is a good time to select a wedge. Because the wedge hits the ball higher, the ball rises quickly, lands quickly, and won't roll as far. Think of the ball in this instance as a helicopter. Up quickly, less roll. Different scenario. When the hole is much farther away, say, thirty feet, a 7-iron, which provides more roll than a wedge, would be an appropriate choice.

There isn't one right answer to the question of which club is best. Think of it this way: The farther away we are from the hole, the less lofted club we use (like a 7-iron) so the ball will roll most of the way. The closer we are to a hole (and the less roll we'll need), we might chose a club with more loft (a wedge or 9-iron).

Know your terms

A quick point of semantics: People often interchange the words pitch and chip. A high shot is always a pitch and a chip is always a low shot that rolls more than it flies.

Trouble Shots

We've all been there. There's nothing like flubbing a chip. More than anything else, chunked chips are the result of tension and going back too quickly. **The more tension, the faster and longer the backswing. If we go back slowly, we'll automatically come through faster. When we swing too fast or too long, we can't help but slow down into the ball.**

It's the traffic equivalent of being broadsided because we couldn't get through the intersection in time. When you flub one, use the miss as a reminder to ease up on the white-knuckle approach. Take a deep breath rather than berate yourself. Sweep that imaginary penny under the ball and step on the gas. I think the most common problem with this shot is simply that people confuse it with the longer full swing rather than the controlled and compact shot that it is.

Checkpoints

Place the clubface behind the ball and aim at the hole.

Look at the hole as you place your feet.

Stand close to the ball with your feet close together and upper arms in close.

Place more weight on the left foot.

Look down at the ball and sweep the grass beneath the ball onto the green.

Remember to step on the gas.

HOW TO PRACTICE

Build a fence with two range buckets and a club laid across the top. Stand about three or four feet back from the green and hit short chips "under the fence." You'll be surprised how many will hop over it.

To save our backs and make it more of a game, hit a chip shot then go up to the green and finish putting the ball into the cup. Hit three shots to different holes, putt out, and try to cut down on the number of strokes.

Another game establishes the sense of touch and distance on

a variety of shots. Chip one ball thirty feet, the next twenty feet, the next ten feet, and then repeat the sequence the other way. Or chip with a friend. The one farthest from the hole retrieves both balls.

This kind of imaginative, playful practice rubs off on our entire game. The better we chip, the better our short games, but also the better our long shots become, too.

The Grip: Grasping the Swing

I'd like to learn the golf swing.
I can't get the ball up in the air.
I play regularly but the ball goes to the right.

It's the key to the golf swing. **Everything happens as a result of the grip.** It determines how far we hit the ball, the ease in getting it off the ground, and whether it finds the target. The grip warrants a whole chapter if only because our hands are the only attachment we have to the golf club.

The consensus in evaluations is that the grip is the hardest fundamental to *get* and the easiest to forget. There is a silver lining. Students arrive with a suspected laundry list of problems. Their swing self-diagnoses are a bit like the patient telling the doctor what to prescribe. Often all it takes to cure a litany of swing ailments is a slight turn of the hands. Such a modest change may seem inconsequential, or feel uncomfortable at first, but after seeing the results even the most skeptical students understand the importance of the placement of the hands.

A sound grip has the bonus of sparing us from a Pandora's box of golf technobabble. We can avoid (brace yourself): swing planes, clubface angles, levels of approach, pronation, release, and wrist cock, to name a few. With a good grip the golf swing flows as easily as a playground swing. When pulled back correctly, each travels efficiently, smoothly, down and through.

I remember a student in a clinic who was dubious about the grip. Stubborn? Well, a little. Our two-hour session was nearly over. It was hot and miserable, and Beverly just could not get the ball in the air with her full swing. Still, she was reluctant to give the instruction a chance. Finally, I placed her hands on the club and again showed her the correct grip.

"It feels so funny," she said.

Eventually, we got Beverly's hands in a good *strong* position on the club, never mind how funny it felt. She hit a ball. It took off, straight with just a touch of draw, or turn to the left at the end. Spontaneous applause broke out among her fellow students.

"Can you live with that?" I asked with a hint of sarcasm.

She could. "It felt so awkward at first," she said, but conceded her new grip "made all the difference." Returning to her spot, Beverly began hitting balls with such enthusiasm one would've thought it was 75° with a cool breeze blowing, instead of a Texas summer afternoon with a heat index of 105°. That's what a good grip will do for you.

Beverly showed a lot of ability and power in her swing, but it was all being lost because of her *weak grip*. Before we broke up, another light bulb went off for someone else. "Yes!" I overheard a student rejoice after a lovely shot. "The grip *does* make all the difference." You better believe it.

Occasional reluctance from students notwithstanding, a good grip shouldn't feel uncomfortable, just the opposite. Unfortunately, a poor grip, once established, can be a difficult habit to break. Changing a grip takes *a lot* of patience and commitment. Golf is so much easier with a grip that's right from the start.

Because of its importance, vigilance about the grip never ends—no matter how experienced the golfer, no matter how often or infrequently one plays. Keeping an eye on it is akin to glancing in a mirror before stepping out or balancing a checking account. Golf with a shaky grip may not be as costly as a bounced check, but it's about as much fun.

The left hand

With the exception of putting and chipping, the golf grip is the same for every swing of the golf club. The grip starts with the vital position of the left hand, perhaps the most important key to good golf you'll read in this, or any other, instruction book. Here's how to get it right:

1. First make sure when holding the club that the bottom rests along the ground; the clubface points towards the target.
2. **Place your left hand on the club so the thumb is on the right side of the grip.** The thumb and index finger will be so close together a penny would be secure between them. In fact, you should feel that your thumb and forefinger are sewn together. This will ensure the club will be more in the fingers than in the palms.

The right hand

After placing the left hand on the club, the right hand is a piece of cake. It merely comes in from the side. The right palm, along the lifeline, fits up against the left thumb. That slot was made for a thumb and a golf grip. The fleshy heel pad of the

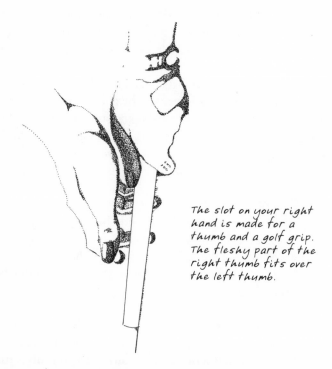

The slot on your right hand is made for a thumb and a golf grip. The fleshy part of the right thumb fits over the left thumb.

right hand covers the left thumb. The right thumb and forefinger should also feel as if they are sewn together.

Grip check

To make sure it's right, with the hands placed properly, three knuckles on the left hand should be visible. You should be able to see the top knuckles of the index, middle, and ring fingers. **Lines formed by the crack where the thumbs and index fingers touch should point to your right shoulder.** Chuck Cook, a former PGA Teacher of the Year, has a handy way of self-appraising a grip. Place a tee between the thumb and forefinger

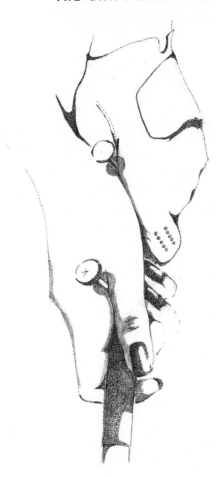

Grip check: With two tees in your pocket, you can check your own grip, anywhere, at any time.

of each hand. Assume your grip. **The tees should point to the right shoulder.** If they point instead to the chin, this is what's known as a "weak grip," and without knowing any more about it, who wants that? To fix a weak grip, turn both hands slightly to the right until the tees line up to that right shoulder. Chuck suggests closing the eyes to get a feel for the grip, then starting over with the eyes open and without the tees.

Backhand

How the hands are placed on top of the club is infinitely more important than what the little fingers are doing in back. Still, they have to go somewhere. There are several options. Those with short, stubby fingers may prefer the interlocking grip (the pinky of the right hand interlocks between the forefinger and middle finger of the left hand). The ten fingered or baseball grip (all ten fingers touching the club) is popular with women with small hands. The overlap grip (the right pinky sits in the space between the left forefinger and middle finger) is probably the most popular of the three. Each is correct. Each has been famously successful.

I recall Harvey saying that the worst thing that can befall a golfer is indecision about grips. Test them out, then come to some resolution. In just about every aspect of golf, the grip included, the worst thing one can be is indecisive.

Fiddling

The hands go on the club without a lot of twisting and turning. Harvey never liked to see golfers "fiddle" with their grips. Place the hands on the club as if it were a dinner fork; hold it in an easy, relaxed way. "Milking" the club, putting and pulling the hands on and off—a close relative to "fiddling"—invites uncertainty.

Pressure gauge

Hold the golf club as if it were a fine musical instrument. Because golf shots are *struck* with a *club* (by rights an object used to smash things), there is an undeniable urge to do just that and, by inference, squeeze the club tightly. One look at a proficient golf swing, however, should dispel that notion.

Lots of images float around for grip "pressure," which itself connotes tension. *Pressure* is not the right word. Some describe holding the club as if it were a small bird. Crushing the poor thing would be inhumane, but we want to make sure she doesn't fall or fly away.

On a scale from one to ten, if one is the consistency of cooked spaghetti (i.e., a very loose grip) and ten is uncooked spaghetti (i.e., rigor mortis), we'd ideally like to be about a six. Dog lovers might imagine they've got an obedient toy poodle on a leash rather than a feisty rottweiler. In both cases, control is our goal, not strangulation, and it's better to err on the looser than the tighter side. When a golfer wants more distance—and who doesn't?—the first requirement is reasonable grip pressure.

It should go without saying that a grip shouldn't hurt. Blisters or "tennis elbow" are red flags that we're holding on too tightly.

Rope burn

For all the care and consideration shown the grip, it can easily slip from its moorings, turning just enough out of position to ravage a swing. What typically happens is the hands want to reach out and grab the club as if it were a rope. It's as if the golfer were preparing to pull herself up a tree, like Jane pursuing Tarzan. The thumbs end up on top of the rope (and on top of the club). Rather than point to the right shoulder, the thumb-and-forefinger line points to the chin. The grip is now "weak." A weak grip is great for rappelling or swinging from vines, but it's perilous for most golfers.

As the grip turns

At the end of every beginning golf school, we play nine holes on a par-three course. One day I was stricken by a Texas-sized allergy attack and had another instructor accompany the group. He came to me afterwards and said he didn't mean to criticize but no one had taught any of the students the correct grip! Despite all the time we'd spent on it, once everybody got out on the golf course, those sound grips evaporated. It happens. The grip is still the hardest fundamental to master.

Coming to grips

I'll give you a perfect example. Having played for years, I was successfully teaching golf when I hit a patch of poor play. Due to poor health, Harvey was then confined to his living room, where he gave many lessons in his declining years.

He listened patiently to my sad tale. The first thing he said was, "Let me see your grip." Then he asked me to check the position of my left hand to be sure all three knuckles showed. I thought they did. "Look again," he said. Could I see three knuckles or two and a half? What's the big deal, right? How important could half a knuckle be? Turning my hand to the right, I realized I had only seen about half of that third knuckle. That was all it took, the difference between hitting the ball crisply and hitting it miserably. Half a knuckle.

I couldn't conceal my disappointment. I was discouraged at my inability to detect my own flaws, but Harvey reminded me that doctors shouldn't be their own patients and lawyers shouldn't be their own clients. It would be nice for our swings, he told me as I was leaving, if we could see for ourselves what others see.

My confidence restored, the experience reminded me of the

fragility of the swing when the grip is even a little "off." Still, I had to marvel. He never saw me hit a shot. So important to a good result, the grip often tips off an instructor to a problem before a student ever hits a ball.

Harvey did warn me that I would occasionally come across golfers who had what we might consider a bad grip. The players had practiced so much that it had become repeatable, no longer a liability. An infrequent player who doesn't often practice would have a much harder time making the adjustments in the two seconds it takes to swing.

All we are saying

Patience is certainly a golfing virtue, but it's especially true with the grip and the persistent urge to choke the ever-loving life out of the club. It's that darn ball again, just sitting there, placidly, waiting for us to do something to it. A good grip can quickly deteriorate under pressure from a natural, even artistic position, into a viselike grip. **Keeping the grip tension free is a lifelong maintenance check.** The best golfers in the world make a conscious effort to open the floodgates and release tension from their bodies—especially their hands—before every shot.

We haven't even taken the club back yet and here I am going on again about relaxation. There are two messages. The first is to **make relaxation part of your routine.** If you're gripping the club any tighter than a fork, that's too much. Be aware of it. Secondly, like any investment, **establishing and changing a grip takes time to bear fruit.** A grip change is a considerable undertaking, in many cases the most difficult transformation a golfer can make. Give it a chance. Remember Beverly, my skeptical student.

When not to change

One last point about the grip before we move onto pitching and the full swing. Just before leaving on a ten-day Hawaiian golf vacation or on the eve of the club championship is definitely *not* the time to effect a grip change. It should be introduced and allowed time to sink in without the added pressure of a trip or competition.

HOW TO PRACTICE

Practice a good grip anywhere, in front of the television if you like. A club is all that's needed. *Place* your hands on the golf club. Look down and count knuckles. Experiment with grip pressure and a couple of tees. Those with calluses are unknowingly turning their hands, moving the skin around, "fiddling," "milking," or gripping the club too tightly, or holding the club more in the palm, instead of the fingers.

CHAPTER
4

Pitching:
The Swing in Miniature

I'm too far from the green to chip.
To avoid trouble, I have to fly my ball to the green.
I want to shoot better scores.

 The pitch shot flies high onto the green and stops fairly quickly. When we can't putt the ball, we chip it. And when we can't chip the ball, we pitch it. Typically we'll use it anywhere from seventy yards in to the green. The pitch is one of the most frequently deployed shots, and plays a major role in how well we score.

Smaller and more compact than the full swing, it's cut from the same cloth and is often thought of as a mini, or abbreviated, swing. The shots are so closely related, problems in the larger swing are often revealed in the pitch. The sand wedge and pitching wedge are the clubs of choice. Don't have one? Use a 9-iron.

Much of what we've learned thus far will help us to hit pitch shots. For instance, like putting and chipping, the pitch has two parts—and only two. All golf swings take two seconds. That's it—despite what you may have read, heard, seen, or been told. One second to go back, one second to swing through. That doesn't leave much time for analysis and contemplation, and that's the way we want it.

How to stand   PITCHING STANCE

We've been over this with our kindergarten exercise. Suffice it to say, an athletic posture is imperative to good golf. Bend at the hips, knees flexed, back straight, swing your "trunk," the arms. Your feet should assume whatever position they'd take if you were just standing watching someone else play. Flare them out slightly, if that's the normal way you stand. Or turn the toes in, if you're slightly pigeon-toed. Whatever's most comfortable.

One way of checking the proper stance is to feel as if your rear end is against a wall. I know there is a reluctance to stick "it" out. Women often comment that for years we've been taught to hold "it" in. Still, this shouldn't be completely foreign. Tennis players will recognize the resemblance of the golf stance to the ready position for returning serve: derrière out, back straight, head up, knees bent, weight centered, ready to move quickly in either direction. Those who play or watch basketball recognize this stance for defense. It's the same pose for a racing dive or getting on a ski lift. The rear end leans out to meet the chair.

A video camera or simply checking yourself in a mirror will confirm the position. I have my students pair up to help each other with the proper grip and stance. It's an enormous plus to have another set of eyes help us with something new.

It seems simple enough, how to stand over a golf ball, but it's an important and sometimes elusive checkpoint. As with all the basics, the stance isn't a "beginner's problem." I'll give you a perfect example. One afternoon on the practice range, my husband was complaining about his pitch shots. He was tinkering with his ball position, talking about making his swing go up more instead of around, and using other manipulations too complicated to go into to try and correct the problem.

I thought I detected a slight change in his stance. (His rear end, small as it is, wasn't out enough.) It wasn't much, but enough—at least to someone who so intimately knows his swing, as I do. Roane dismissed my mention of it with, "It's the way I've always stood over the ball."

Thanks to a handy video camera, a few surreptitiously filmed swings turned up that afternoon on the VCR. I never said a word. Roane came into the room, saw the clips, said something that sounded like "good grief," and excused himself to go to the driving range. He later confessed he couldn't believe what had happened. He's an attorney, played on the University of Texas golf team, tried the pro tour and has won many amateur tournaments, including the Austin City Championship five times. His playing accomplishments are cited only to underscore how easy it is, even for an experienced player, to lose sight of something so basic.

There is a tendency to stand up as we pitch, and it's an easy thing to overlook during the course of a round. **The knees have to stay flexed throughout the swing.** Straightening the knees lifts the club above the ball and causes topped shots. Reviewing the stance is akin to ticking off a key ingredient in a recipe.

Holding the club   PITCHING GRIP

The previous chapter goes into the grip in some detail. Suffice it to say, a relaxed grip is also essential to a pitch shot. The more relaxed the hands are, the easier they feel the weight of the club.

Tension eliminates this delicate sense of touch.

With something as long as a golf club, there is a temptation to hold it well away from the body. The arms should instead extend straight down (*à la* swinging the elephant's trunk) and that's where the club is gripped.

To play a pitch shot, line up the hands even with the inside of your left thigh. The clubhead will then address the ball in the middle of your feet.

Where the ball goes   BALL POSITION

With the hands inside the left thigh, the ball is then in the middle of the stance. This is a ball position we'll use over and over with other shots.

A feel for pitching

So much of golf boils down to *feel,* a sometimes elusive way of describing the instinctive athletic and artistic movements we do without a second thought. We need to develop that kind of deep understanding to learn and trust this shot.

To get a feel for pitching, scatter several tees on the ground in a row in front of you, a foot or so apart. Aim the leading edge of the golf club behind a tee toward a target: a green on the range, or a tree in the backyard. Now, sweep a tee away and then step up to the next one and sweep it away and so on until you reach the end of the line. No need to stop after each one to adjust your blouse, check the wind conditions, consult with other golfers, or ponder the position of the tee. Move casually from one to the next, sweeping the tees with a short stroke. Notice that your feet move as you swing as if you were sweeping a floor, moving slightly back then slightly forward. This may not seem revelatory, but you're experiencing the weight shift crucial to hitting a golf ball, and doing it without thinking.

Here's the athletic
stance for a pitch shot:
relaxed, knees flexed,
good posture with the
back.

If we're not worrying about golf, we'll stand as we should (or pretty close) to optimally sweep the tees. And if we missed one the first time, we'd just sweep it again without analyzing the position of the elbows or the angle of the wrists. We also won't worry about whether our stance is too wide or too narrow. We just sweep. This free swinging at tees conveys exactly what the pitch shot feels like.

Brush Strokes
Sweeping tees has other merits:

1. It automatically gives us a desirable slow backswing and faster follow-through.
2. It conveys the motion of the golf swing.
3. If we miss a few we'll automatically make the needed adjustment. We'll swing lower or stand closer. (It's noteworthy that students never ask what they are doing wrong when they miss a tee or fail to get it up in the air; only with a ball.)

We'll go on to describe the shot in some detail, but all you may need to learn the short pitch shot is to think of sweeping tees.

Now do it with a ball
Those who can easily sweep tees or pennies (without being concerned about where they go) and do it well sometimes experience problems switching to balls. This should be a breeze; after all, the tees and pennies are much smaller than a golf ball. Staring at the ball, however, personalities change, expectations kick in, and our swings get bigger. We're suddenly overcome with the urge to *hit* instead of *sweep*. And, most of all, we want that ball

up in the air. **Feel the ball being hit before looking up to see what happened.** Sweep the grass clippings out from beneath the ball and it will take off like a mallard leaving a pond.

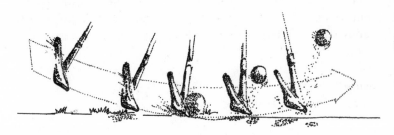

Clip the spot directly under the ball.

Weeding

The difficulty in pitching comes from an inclination to lift the ball to *help* it go high in the air. In fact, the opposite is true. **To hit the ball high we swing low.** The correct swing is the one that clips the tee (penny or grass) directly under the ball as it sweeps it out to the range. The ball thus becomes an incidental part of the swing.

If none of the above works, imagine a snake lying in wait directly beneath the ball. As you swing make sure to lop off its head or it will pop up and bite. Perhaps a little extreme, as examples go, but those with a fear of snakes will relate.

One of Harvey's favorite teachers, Percy Boomer, whose book *On Learning Golf* has been in print since the early 1940s, had a good way of thinking about the pitch swing. He suggested feeling as if we were driving a wedge under a door rather than hammering a nail into the ground.

Carry that weight

We've covered the short pitch, but the longer pitch shot more closely approximates the full swing.

First, we'll add an element that will reflect positively on your whole game. **The swing starts by turning and simultaneously placing weight on the inside of the right foot.** This is essential to a consistent, balanced swing. Bracing on the right instep with the knees flexed as we turn anchors the swing, allowing us to turn rather than slide. It also keeps us centered over the ball so that the swing that goes back (one) can return precisely to the ball when quickly swinging through (two).

Howdy. Howdy.

This longer swing brings the club back farther and requires a longer follow-through. As the weight goes to the instep, we simultaneously turn away from the ball. Think of it as turning to shake hands with someone on either side.

First without a club, assume your stance. Pretend you're in a dollhouse and that if you stood up, you'd bump your head. Those inclined to car repair can imagine being under the hood. This is simply to maintain good posture, keeping the head still. Resist the penchant to stand up during the swing. The knees remain flexed, the back straight.

Turn the shoulders back as you reach to shake hands, first with someone on your right and then around to someone standing on your immediate left. Shake with the left hand going back and the right hand coming through. Bring the hands up about waist height.

Or, try this: Picture your body as a clock. If the head is 12:00 and the feet 6:00, swing the arms back from 3:00 to 9:00.

Another way of visualizing this is to imagine standing be-tweeen two boxes. Avoid touching the boxes when swinging the club back. This is important. Moving straight back, the swing can continue unfettered as it travels back and up. You can also recognize this concept by standing alongside a sofa. Place your right leg against the arm of the sofa. By swinging an imaginary club straight back, notice that you miss the sofa as the swing lengthens and goes up. Both these exercises em-phasize the need to swing back straight in leaving the ball. That's the key.

How far, and a quick physics lesson

How far back should the swing go? That depends on the shot. Let's go back out to the yard. If I'm going to sweep grass just off the walk, I'll barely take the broom back. About to toss a ball to a nearby child, or toss a scrap of paper into the wastebasket, same thing—the arm barely comes back. To toss the ball farther, the arm comes back farther. **The length of the backswing controls the length of the shot.**

Since the swing is one-two, on the way back you'll know if you've gone too far. No stopping in midswing, though. Get to two. It's the most important part of the shot. However far the club comes back, it should go forward at least that far, the same as a child's playground swing or a porch swing.

An abrupt stop at the bottom of the swing is akin to dumping a child onto the ground. The golf swing has to be allowed to finish. That's one of the reasons Harvey never liked to see a prac-tice swing cut short. If a swing goes back (and virtually one hun-dred percent of us can take the club back without any problem) it *must* swing quickly to the other side.

Some swings stop or slow down, the golfer figuring that it's over once the club strikes the ball. Others swing a little past and stop. The ball's been hit, where'd it go? These are logical responses, but golf isn't always logical. The ball's on its way. There's no reason to keep going, right? Wrong. Remember Mrs. Lovejoy, the race car driver. Once the club comes back, it's time to step on the gas and get that ball out of the intersection. **Remember, two has to be as far through as one was back.**

Studies show

Ninety percent of pitch shots are missed because golfers slow down at the ball or fail to clip enough grass under it. The faster the backswing, the more insistent the message from the brain to slow down into the ball. The reverse should be the case: A slow backswing followed by a faster follow-through.

Apprehension and anxiousness to see the results of the shot often spoil it. Uncertainty, anxiety, and tension stop the club from swinging through smoothly. Instead of getting through the intersection, we stall out in it.

This shot never has a real long backswing, but it *always* has a full follow-through. If you feel you need a longer swing, or more distance, change out the wedge for a 9-iron. It won't fly quite as high, but the ball will sail and roll farther.

The Finish

To produce a good shot, the swing must be completed. It must get to two. It must finish. Otherwise, it's only a work in progress, and the result will be a ball that's topped, skulled, or short of the green.

The finish mimics the backswing, but accelerating through

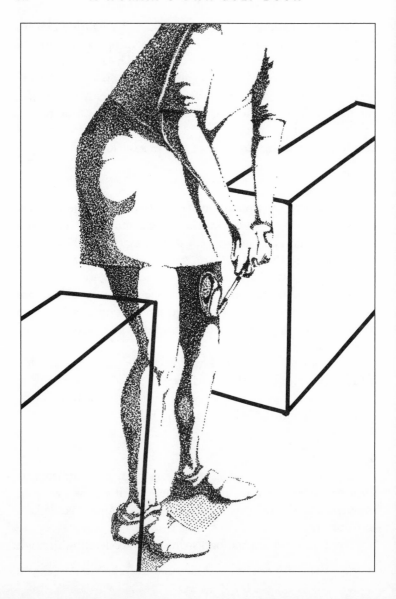

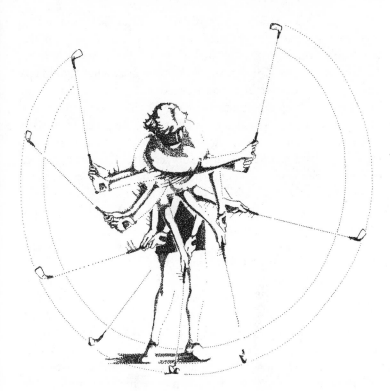

Remember to look at the ball as you shake hands and say hello to your right and shake hands and say hello to your left.

the ball makes the end of the swing longer. It happens so quickly. Stepping on the gas should also help us finish facing the target.

Swing analysis

Books have been written about the pitch shot. Here's a word of advice. Golfers tend to look at the game as being so technical that everything warrants an explanation. Television commentators do their part. If you ever watch tournament golf on the weekends, announcers offer analysis worthy of a space launch. Acclaimed teacher Rick Smith jokes that a disclaimer should appear on the screen when announcers pause to scrutinize a swing.

"Let's look at that pitch of Tiger Woods," one might say during a lull in the action. "He's hit it over the green from sixty yards out. In slow motion, notice the hip turn, the wrist cock, the swing plane, shaft plane, and clubface angle. See the dynamics of the clubface orientation and the inside path of the shaft plane? Oops, there it is, the clubface is closed at impact. Even though the swing path is to the right, the spin caused the ball to curve left and long. Don't you agree, Bob?"

"Absolutely. That inside take-away caused the shaft angle to come into the impact zone too steeply, requiring more rotation. . . ." And so it goes.

What do *I* think? I think he needed to take a shorter backswing and swing easier.

Against a cascading river of information that flows through the game's consciousness fed by television, magazines, books, friends, CD-ROMs, etc., the uninitiated can find themselves at a definite disadvantage. But while it may seem that worlds divide the new and experienced golfer, often their problems are quite similar. The biggest difference is that newcomers display their faults more flagrantly and frequently. The way the game is taught continues to evolve—and it may often seem unnecessarily complex—but, the fundamentals never vary.

Checkpoints
Take your grip.
Aim the clubface at the target, placing your feet as you do so.

The hands fall just inside the left thigh.
Look at the target as long as you like.
Look at the ball no longer than three seconds.
Shake hands on the backswing.
Clip the grass under the ball as you step on the gas.
Shake hands with the target.

HOW TO PRACTICE

Start out by hitting balls with a short backswing. Then gradually make longer swings. This will build familiarity with the length of the backswing required for different distances.

Practicing these shots will improve your entire game, not just pitching. The pitch is a precursor to the longer, full swing. Hitting that spot underneath the ball (remember the snake!) is required for every shot except putting and bunker play. The more skilled you become at it, the lower your scores will be.

To underscore the value of the pitch shot, Tom Kite has become one of the all-time best wedge players.

Tom was skilled athletically as a boy, and he's always enjoyed practicing. He's never looked upon improving his golf as "work." To those who watch him spend hours on the practice range hitting pitch shots—even after he "made it"—his efforts may seem like work, but they're not, at least not to Tom.

There's nothing novel in saying it, but when we enjoy applying ourselves, whatever the task, time passes quickly. Make your practice more interesting, more captivating, more entertaining, more fun. Time permitting, approach it as Tom does. And when you miss a few, forget them. Don't let a few bad shots make you more careful. Use those misses as a reminder to relax.

CHAPTER
5

The Two-Second Swing

I'm developing a golf swing.
I'm not hitting the ball solidly.
I'm hitting my wedges okay but not my irons.

Tension, fear, anxiety, trepidation, misgivings, dread, pressure, apprehension, indecision, worry, doubt, expectation. The full swing can summon the forces of the dark side. They conspire to make us straighten up, top it, slice it, or accelerate several blocks before the intersection. For some people it's public speaking or city driving, but for golfers, nothing gets the pulse racing like the unpredictability of the golf swing.

But what's the worst that can happen? The absolute pits would be to completely miss the ball. Embarrassing as that may be, on the golf course it's actually *better* than hitting it in the water or out of bounds because we avoid a penalty. Needless to say, a *whiff* is not what we have in mind, but it's not as far off from being a good shot as it appears. Swinging and missing also tells me that the student is not slowing down into the ball, a definite plus. Slowing down is one cause of hitting the ground before the ball.

Even when the results aren't exactly terrific, swings are routinely better than they look. It goes back to us not being able to see what we're doing.

"Good swing," I'll say in passing, often surprising students with a compliment.

"Who, *me?*" They turn, astonished.

"The difference between a good shot and a bad shot," novelist John Updike recognized, "was marvelously large, and yet the difference between a good swing and a bad seemed microscopically small." That's a perfect summation of why golfers sweat the small stuff.

In a way, golf swings are like gardens. Both need regular upkeep and time to thrive. Rest assured, if we get lax, hitches will infest our swings like cutworms in the vegetables. And once we learn the fundamentals, we can't assume that's that. In this respect, golf is more like riding a horse than a bike. Continually monitor the grip, stance, aim, and alignment, and never take them for granted. Like preparing to go horseback riding, before climbing into the saddle, we always secure the stirrups and bridle. For all its difficulty, the full swing is merely a longer pitch shot. We've covered nearly all of the components in learning to chip and pitch. Now we'll pull them together.

One stretch

Despite what its detractors may say, golf remains an athletic endeavor (more so, of course, when walking). Warming up the swing is as important as loosening up the body, and there's a stretch I heartily recommend that helps both. It's wonderful for

Pull your arm out to the side as far as you can, then pull it up. Try and get your left shoulder under your chin with the right elbow pointing down and the weight on the right instep.

improving the flexibility to make a full shoulder turn and for conveying the feel of the ideal backswing. Ninety percent of it will be familiar to you from turning to shake hands on a pitch shot.

First, take your stance. Let the arms hang freely. Grasp your left wrist with your right hand, thumb on top. Pull the left arm across the body to shoulder height. It's as if you're reaching to shake hands with someone on your right using your left hand. Turn your shoulders to stretch to the side. Try and pull the left shoulder under the chin. Then pull the hands up a little higher. Hold it right there. That's the backswing.

As the left arm is pulled to the side, the right arm folds and the elbow points to the ground. An easier way to think of this is to keep the elbows close together as you stretch.

The knees stay flexed throughout and until the very end of the swing. It's as if you were standing in an attic. Try not to bump your head on the low ceiling. Hold that athletic pose. Like a door, the golf swing opens and closes on the same level, back one way then the other. Remember to look at the ground as if a ball were there. All this is simply to help you maintain good posture during the swing.

Practice the full swing with a 6- or 7-iron. Which club?

Moo!   **FULL SWING GRIP**

A gentle reminder to grip the club lightly. Let tension out of the elbows and shoulders. Place the hands on the club and leave them there. Refrain from *milking* it.

I once gave lessons to a piano teacher who said that she related to everything I was saying about relaxation. While listening to me, she could almost hear herself emphasizing good posture and the importance of releasing tension from the elbows and shoulders, fingers and hands, to her students. Carol said learning golf gave her more empathy for her aspiring pianists. It reminded her of the difficulty in combatting tension. As odd as it sounds, relaxing is something we just have to work on, at the piano or with the golf swing.

Shoulder width   **FULL SWING STANCE**

A good stance allows you to get close to the ball, arms hanging comfortably, just as in the pitch shot. **The insides of the heels should be shoulder-width apart.** Body types largely determine the stance, and, really, the character of the swing. In the same way that each of us walk differently, the golf swing differs individually. The tall and supple may have a wider stance while shorter players with limited flexibility may stand with their feet closer together. Generally, for all shapes and sizes on shorter shots, the stance instinctively narrows.

Hello, ball   **BALL POSITION**

The ball should be played in the middle of the stance.

The hands should be inside the left thigh. Stand close enough to the ball to avoid having to reach out to hit it. Topped shots are often caused by standing too far from the ball or by straightening the knees during the swing. Think of the elephant walk.

One:

Women would never hit the ball very far if they depended on strength alone. Look at the builds of good golfers, of either sex. They're not muscle-bound. **The golf swing is a product of relaxation that permits flexibility and speed to occur.**

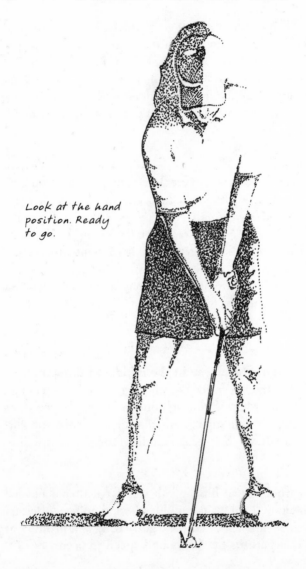

Look at the hand position. Ready to go.

Remember the children's game—we called it "crack the whip"—where kids link hands and spin? Same principle. The more kids in the line, the longer the chain, and the more speed generated for the whip. The daredevil on the end of the chain (the one whose feet leave the ground and whose knees get badly scraped) goes the fastest because he's the beneficiary of all that speed. That's why the longer the club, the more speed generated, thus, the further we hit the ball. The line isn't turning very fast but there's a lot of speed being realized out on the end. Envision the child on the end of the whip as your clubhead.

On the full swing, the shoulders turn well away from the ball, as far as they comfortably can. You can even feel like you're taking the club back with your shoulders. The turn is what stores and then delivers speed.

Weight right here

When turning, as with the pitch shot, the weight shifts to the inside of the right foot. This provides the body with an anchor and balances the swing. Get comfortable feeling the weight there. Allowing the weight to roll to the outside of the foot is positively lethal, as any gymnast who works on the balance beam or any good golfer will tell you.

How far back do I go? SHOULDER TURN

There is a definite benchmark to the length of the backswing. **Turn back as in our stretch—until the shoulders can't go any farther.** The golf swing looks like it's all arms and elbows. The truth is the less flexible we are the more arms we use, and when the arms outrun the shoulders, they swing through on their own, powerless. Overswinging, we lose our snap.

A full shoulder turn is imperative to a good swing. That's where the power comes from. Taking the club back slowly gives the big muscles of the back and shoulders time to turn. Again, feel as if the shoulders are taking the club back.

Some of us are admittedly more flexible than others. A golfer with broad shoulders may not make as full a turn as someone with narrow shoulders. An older man will not have the flexibility of a young woman. The less flexible, whether because of age or body type, still use the same benchmarks. The swing (or arms) stopping when the shoulders stop turning will still produce more power than a long arm swing. You may be more flexible than you think. Turn and look behind you and you'll find the shoulders adequately turn.

Two

Be fearless. Swing decisively to two. Trust your stance, grip, aim, turn, alignment, ability. Swing the club until it stops of its own accord.

Let's have some of that "killer" instinct. Swing through until your (insert one or more as needed) belt buckle, navel, breasts, right shoulder, elbows completely turn to face the target. Your hands should end up by your left ear, your right foot should be up on its toe high enough that the sole can be seen by someone behind you.

Pay attention to what you look like at the end of the swing because it tells the story of what came before. And look admiringly at that lovely shot you've hit. Even if it was not quite so lovely, we're going to look like we've hit a lovely shot by completely turning. The full swing is an all or nothing proposition. Let it go. Give it a chance to happen. If you'll just let that club go, it'll go right to two. **Feel the ball leave before you look up to see it.**

Regardless of what happens, I would much rather see golfers throw caution to the wind by *finishing* without stopping or slowing down. **The swing that slows down will never produce a pleasurable shot.** With their knees flexed—and students thinking about clipping the tee or the grass beneath it—those who completely missed the ball a few seconds before will hit a good shot with that same swing.

New golfers are often overly cautious, approaching the swing tentatively, modestly, like a dip in the ocean, the golfer wading in one extremity at a time. Perhaps this stems from the feminine penchant for perfection. We want to do things right with a demure sense of reserve, with proper planning and preparation.

This is when, in the same breath that I have to remind men that "golf is not a violent game," I tell women, as politely as I can, "Kill it!" Some women don't want to hurt the grass or worry about scarring it. I'll never forget the student who, staring at the hole she created with a ferocious swing, it was all she could do to look on the bright side. Gazing mournfully at that impressive divot, she said: "You know, I could plant a tulip in that." She wasn't kidding.

Yes, we want to sweep the club back slowly, in the same way we use a flyswatter, pull back the playground swing, or back the car out of the garage. But once the club has gone back in control, swing through with authority. Instead of putting a toe in the water, dive in headfirst.

Harvey's bucket

Harvey taught the full swing with a bucket of water. The secret to swinging a pail without spilling is to sweep it back by starting slowly, gradually building momentum. Swing the club as if there's a bucket of water on the end.

If you ever come across the phrase "let the club do the work," this is what it refers to: After we've swept the club/bucket back, we then let centrifugal force do the rest.

My English friend Barry Dixon has a good image of the swing. Ideally, it follows the path of a saucer rather than up and down the sides of a teacup. We want an airplane taking off and landing with our swing, not a helicopter; a saucer, not a teacup; a broom, not a hammer.

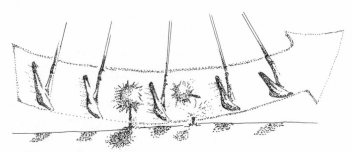

Clip what's underneath: a tee, a blade of grass, a dandelion. Whatever image works.

Clip the tee

At the moment of truth, clip the tee, or the grass under the ball. The faster the swing through, the longer the follow-through, and the longer the shot. **Clipping the tee makes us do so many things right without having to think of anything else.** If you really want to know, it squares the clubface, matches the low point of the swing at the ball, and promotes swinging through rather than lifting up. All good things come from clipping that tee.

It's analogous to my interest in cars. Although I certainly admire those who understand all the technology involved in internal combustion engines and respect those responsible for its design, I'm not terribly concerned with the intricacies of electronic ignition, only with whether my car is running smoothly.

With the golf swing, there's only so much we need to know, and in two seconds, how much can we mull over or discuss with ourselves?

As Bobby Jones so eloquently wrote: "The more one fiddles around arranging the position, the more likely one is to be beset by doubts that produce tension and strain."

Ahead of the game

How many times has someone told you to keep your head down? Good advice in the trenches, it's from that long list of golf clichés. Anxious to see what happens, golfers often look up too soon. **Stay in that athletic position and look down at the ball until it's long gone, at least until the club is waist high on the follow-through.** During the course of a normal swing, the head stays level. It may move slightly to the right, but never up or down. You should feel at the end of the swing as if you are still bent over, that it's the momentum of the club swinging through that ultimately brings you back upright.

We're only human

Misconceptions about the swing abound in part, because it's so hard to tell what we're doing. The result is that **ninety-five percent of golfers swing back too far.** I may be underestimating. The brain tells us to reach back as far as we can. The problem is that the backswing doesn't hit anything. Since we can't see what we're doing and because it seems logical, we take the club back too far and too fast, thus wasting energy and losing balance. Percy Boomer noted that we lose rhythm as soon as we hurry, and we hurry as soon as we are afraid.

Overwind a top or a music box, what happens? The top won't spin and the music won't play. Same with the golf swing. Go back too far and momentum is squandered when it should carry us through the ball.

A photo finish

After the swing, having reached that beautiful high finish, pretend a photographer is taking your picture. This was a Harvey trick to get golfers to "hold it" for a second, as if posing in front of a camera. It serves as another reminder to fully complete the swing.

Taking your swing to the golf course

Establishing a routine before each shot is one of those measures of consistency of a good game. The value is in being able to organize one's thoughts and emotions to repeat the swing. Preshot routines vary. Here are the essential elements:

Survey the shot from behind the ball. This offers the best view of the hole. Pick out a specific target. Step up to the ball and put the club behind it, taking aim. Move the feet into position and take a stance. Look at the target as long as you like, but when you look down at the ball, go—hit it—within two seconds, three seconds max.

Checklist

Take your grip and aim the clubface where you want to go.

Look at the green or fairway and place your feet.

Focus on the target as long as you like.

But look down at the ball for just a moment or two before you . . .

Swing!

One: Turn the shoulders away from the ball and swing back slowly.

Two: Crisply clip the grass or the tee on your way through.

This tells the story of what came before. Complete every swing. Finish what you started.

HOW TO PRACTICE

Spending a few minutes chipping and putting before going to the range loosens up the small muscles in preparation for the full swing. And it practices hitting the exact spot beneath the ball so crucial to longer shots.

I once overheard an instructor say that more learning is done without the ball. This may be true. Without the bother of a ball, make several *complete* slow-motion swings to develop a sense of coordination and feel. Practice the stretch and the full turn of the shoulders while shifting your weight to the right instep. One. Two.

On the range practice with a tee. Hit balls with a wedge or 9-iron and alternate back and forth with the 6- or 7-iron. Tee the ball up fairly high. This will help instill the rhythm of the shot before teeing it lower or playing it off the grass. We need to walk before we can run. Students often feel as if they're somehow cheating by hitting range balls off a tee, but this is rehearsal, and clipping the tee makes so many good things happen.

It also promotes one thing we'll keep to a whisper, that we're hitting down on the ball. It's really the worst advice. We hear "down" and interpret it to mean hammer into nail. Concentrate instead on clipping the tee. It brings the club to its lowest point, where it should be—underneath the ball—before starting up. Pretend you're clipping off dandelion heads.

Play a game of tee limbo. After clipping three tees in a row out from under a ball, lower the tee slightly. How low can you go? Each time you easily clip three straight, keep pushing it down until the tee's at grass level. This is how you learn to hit it off the ground. Just imagine a small tee is under every golf ball.

Generously wide, the driving range can mask inaccuracy. Practice your aim by lining up to a specific target. Laying a club on the ground aimed at the target will help.

I'm reminded of a student who was in such a hurry to learn golf that he skipped over the alignment chapter in an instruction book. He figured aiming would be easy. He came back for lessons when his ball never went where he wanted. Alignment is so important. I've watched Tom Kite spend hours making sure he was lined up exactly. It can mean the difference between hitting the bull's eye or missing the target altogether.

Swinging the Woods

What can I do to get more distance?
Can you help me hit the ball farther
  (and more accurately)?
Did I mention I'd like more distance?

 During a golf school in Dallas, I noticed at the end of the range a gentleman holding a woman's arm and swinging the club back for her. Since he wasn't enrolled in the class, I assumed he was merely being helpful, if intrusive. It was apparent things weren't going well.

Years of teaching and answering letters from unsettled *Golf for Women* magazine readers has given me some insight into questions of decorum between golf couples. No stranger to these sorts of issues at home, they remain close to my heart.

So Miss Manners strolled over to impart some kindly advice. Learning the swing and marital happiness, I was about to say, are not mutually exclusive when the man cut me off. He began lecturing me, going on about his wife's swing not having enough wrist cock. To say he was impolite would be like suggesting jalapeños are hot. I managed to get in that I teach a strong grip so the wrists cock without students having to concern themselves. I was sure she'd get it right, I said. He would have none of it, however, and walked off.

"I don't care if she knows it or not," he shouted over his shoulder, "she *still* needs *more* wrist cock!"

Turning to the poor woman, I said, "Let me give you some advice in dealing with your husband and enjoying golf."

She looked at me strangely. "Husband! I don't even know him!"

Here a complete stranger had interrupted my golf school and picked off one of my students like a sniper. Despite his manners I suppose his intentions were honorable. What else can you say? Another time the guy on the driving range tractor began to "teach" the class.

These war stories won't come as any great surprise to women, but there's got to be more in play here than meets the eye, some deep-seeded chivalrous impulse. It may be that the full swing, especially the woods, triggers an instinctive reflex in men, emitting a faint feminine distress signal that they simply find irresistible.

The desire with the woods, of course, is for distance. *Everyone* wants more of it, newcomers right up to experienced players who absolutely crave an extra five yards.

Metals?

Calling them woods is something of a misnomer. Different metal alloys have all but replaced persimmon and other hardwoods as the main ingredient in drivers and fairway clubs. By any name, however, these clubs are longer than the others. The

On the tee, in the fairway, even in the sand, the ball and hand position will be like this.

extra inch or so places us farther away from the ball, and that affects our timing. It also allows us to generate more momentum.

Because of their added length, woods can be difficult to hit, but **regardless of the club in our hands, the swing remains the same.**

The fundamentals haven't changed. They're still our blueprint. **Swinging a wood requires the same shoulder turn as a 5-iron, a 7-iron, or a pitching wedge. A strong grip and shifting the weight to the right instep in turning are just as important as ever.**

We may have a favorite club, but familiarity with different clubs is the first step towards consistency and improvement. I remember a student once telling Harvey, "I can hit my 7-iron, but I can't hit my 3-wood." His reply was typical. "Pretend your 3-wood is your 7-iron." Next lesson. With today's prices not many teachers could get away with that, but stories like these just add to the legend. Harvey never charged much anyway. When a golfer could hit a 3-wood well, only then would he suggest moving up to a driver.

"Just pretend it's a 3-wood," he'd say.

Golf is a mental game, for sure. Of course, there's nothing wrong with pretending a 3-wood is a 7-iron—if it puts you at ease.

Start with a 3-wood

The longest club in the bag, the driver is also the hardest to hit. That's why I would much rather see you start, and get comfortable, with a 3- or 5-wood first. Harvey would take the driver away from anyone having trouble hitting it and tell them to just put it in the trunk or leave it in their closet to avoid any temptation. He'd even grab it right out of their bags.

Been there   **WOODS STANCE**

For the woods, we still want a stance that maintains a straight back and bends at the hips. Knees slightly flexed allow the arms to freely hang with the shoulders relaxed.

Where to put it   **BALL POSITION**

Because the 3-wood is longer than the irons (though not as long as a driver), stand with the ball a couple of ball-widths left of center. Line up so the ball is even with the left heel.

What to do with the hands

We're standing with the ball slightly ahead of where we've had it for other shots. Still the hands stay just inside the left thigh, the same place they've always been.

With this shot there is a tendency to stand too far from the ball. This forces us to reach out to it because the club feels so long in our hands. Probably the same lesson has been given to thousands of golfers having trouble getting woods in the air. Standing an inch closer to the ball often solves the problem.

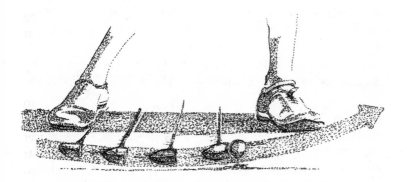

How high is the ball teed up?

Tee it up so half of the ball shows above the clubhead with the club placed behind it. Try teeing the ball higher if you're having trouble getting it into the air.

Going up

With the woods, the ball is played closer to the left foot, the front of our stance. This enables us to hit the ball on the way up as the club comes through and get it in the air faster. Teeing up the ball also facilitates this. Think of the airplane taking off and landing.

We still need that low, slow take-away instructors love to talk about. In fact, we need it more than ever, since it will take us a hair longer to make our backswing because of the added length of the club. This can tempt us into picking up the golf club and taking it back too fast and too far. The cure is our full-swing stretch.

The swing happens so quickly, and the pros swing so smoothly, to the untrained eye it looks like one second the club is on the ground and the next it's up in the air. Closer inspection reveals the pros slowly sweep it back. Picking up the club shortens the swing. And what abruptly goes up abruptly comes down. Chopping at the ball leads to *skying* it and getting hardly any distance. The result is that shallow pop-up that looks like a pitch shot instead of a drive. The antidote? Sweep the ball. Clip the tee.

Keep the head down?

Back to the old saw about keeping your head down, one of any number of panaceas offered up by the well-meaning who aren't sure what else to say but feel they have to say something.

Here's how long to look down at the ball (although we can't

Feel yourself in this position on every shot. Feel it before you see it.

think of it during the swing). When the club is about hip- or waist-high on the follow-through (the ball, of course, is on its way), it's time to see where it's going, for the obvious reason that we'll soon have to find it. **Keep the head up and steady, allow the shoulders to turn. Feel the shot being hit before looking up to see it.**

Step on it

Like the full swing, the drive is all or nothing, pedal to the metal. Stifle the instinct to be extra careful and cautious. That's fine as far as the backswing's concerned, but when you get to one, get to two as fast as you can. Slowing down results in a shorter shot. Don't let a few misses deter your determination to have speed in your swing. I'd rather see you swing and miss. At least you're not hitting the ground. The swing that hits the ground before the ball is slowing down.

With a capital T

Tee shots could fill several annals of golf psychology. We've all seen people wind up and swing like Mighty Casey, preparing to boom one into the next county. And miss. There's the pressure of everyone watching compounded by the shot's difficulty. The green is a blip on the horizon, the air is thick with nervous energy.

Loneliness on the tee has been likened to being at sea in a rowboat. Everyone gets butterflies on the tee, pros included. We wouldn't be human if we didn't. Better players deal with it by making relaxation before every shot as much a part of their routine as checking the wind. They know the constricting nature of tension. These feelings may be intensified for women finding their way in a game long a male preserve, but pressure is definitely *not* a gender issue. Neither is distance.

The trouble with Harry

The value and simplicity of the fundamentals was brought home to me by a lesson I gave to a student we'll call "Harry." (This name has been changed to protect the innocent.)

Harry was a good player who told me over the phone he was having trouble with his driver. Right-brain, Type A, an engineer, however you describe him, Harry was a technical person who expected technical instruction. It didn't take him long to realize he'd come to the wrong place.

"Clip that tee under the ball," I suggested as he began practicing with the 3-wood. He did and hit a terrific shot.

"Just think of clipping that tee beneath the ball and nothing else," I repeated. He was hitting beauties.

His response, however, was less than enthusiastic.

"I can't believe I'm paying for this," he said. After a few more good shots he said it again. I could see him thinking: "Since I spent good money on this, I might as well go along with her." He left soon after and I never saw or heard from him again.

Funny thing was, months later, I got a call from a gentleman interested in scheduling a private lesson. In the course of our conversation, it turned out he'd been referred to me by, of all people, Harry.

"He said you were the best instructor in town," Ted told me. You could have knocked me over with a feather. Harry had a good swing. All he really needed was to focus on the simplest thing, clipping the tee. Instead he was thinking about everything else but. Over time I think he realized the value of keeping it simple.

More distance guaranteed!

Now that I've got your attention . . . golfers of all abilities have a preoccupation with distance that, to put it mildly, borders on obsession.

Let's be realistic. Few of us who lustily belt it out in the shower will ever challenge Ella Fitzgerald or Barbra Streisand. The world's most accomplished vocal coach on an unlimited budget couldn't get us there. Some people just have the talent to hit it farther. Others have the talent to sing. That doesn't mean we can't enjoy ourselves.

It won't happen overnight, but every golfer can hit it longer. First, go back to basics, fitness basics.

When the golf teaching community gathers, there are perennial calls for heightened awareness of the importance of fitness and physical well-being. Golf instructors share the blame. Endlessly fascinated with the mechanics of the swing, we lose sight of what makes it run.

Point of order: We could all be in better shape. **Improving your flexibility will improve your golf.** Any regular exercise will have a positive effect on your stamina, flexibility, and distance. Start with our shoulder stretch. **Swinging a weighted club is another golf-specific exercise to increase distance.** There are various products that will also help; one's called the Distance Doughnut. Nothing fancy, it slips on a club and can be swung (without a ball) in the backyard or on the range. We're talking very inexpensive, under $10. The idea is to build what Harvey called "golf muscles." Once the weight's removed, the club feels so much lighter, we're able to swing it faster. Simply bulking up is undesirable for golf.

Sporting goods stores stock a variety of hand strengtheners. This is not, I repeat, *not* to help us grip the club any tighter, but to maintain speed through the swing and keep the club from turning. There's one like Silly Putty called Power Putty, along with foam cutouts and probably a dozen others. Keep one in the car and squeeze it at red lights, or at your desk while on hold.

Another exercise is to turn a golf club upside down and, holding the club end, swing the grip end as fast as you can. Huh? Do it and you'll hear that lovely *swoosh* as you swing, just as you come down to where the ball would be. Really make it loud by stepping on the gas. Learning to make that *swoosh* will increase the speed of the swing. Listen for it and recognize how fast to swing to reproduce that same sound with a ball and clubhead.

A correct stance, a strong grip, a full shoulder turn, keeping the weight on the inside of the right foot, that's the recipe for improved distance—and accuracy. Swing with relaxed elbows and shoulders and *swoosh* to "two."

The pros, men and women, are regularly surveyed for their insights on gaining distance. Tom Kite recommends making sure the backswing "is really slow so you can apply the power." A sampling of other professional opinions: stay relaxed; take a bigger shoulder turn (which, incidentally, you'll get with better flexibility); make the swing wider and slower; and make a tighter turn, winding up like a coil.

A final thought in the pursuit of distance: Before trying to increase it, increase your percentage of solid shots. A mishit or misdirected shot often costs more distance than one realizes.

Fairway woods

Hitting a wood without a tee is one of the most exacting shots in golf. Learn it first with a 5- or 7-wood. After you feel comfortable with these clubs, you'll be able to progress to a 3-wood. The ball will be closer to your left foot than your right, and the hands will be just inside the left thigh. There is nothing new in this swing.

Thinking about it makes me appreciate even more noted teacher Butch Harmon's observation that "All golfers want to hit the ball farther, and most want to hit it even farther than they can." The inherent difficulty of the fairway woods encourages an overly long backswing. Butch's note is included here because with fairway woods, the club has to swing through the ball quite level. An out of control backswing typically comes down on top of the ball. To successfully hit this shot, the club has to have a level approach into the ball, like our proverbial airplane. As the plane lands, it stays on the runway a short distance (just long enough to hit the ball) before taking off again.

Start by teeing up a ball and sweeping it off the tee. Gradually lower the tee until it's at ground level. Keep sweeping. It's a challenge to keep the club coming in low rather than down and up. One tip is to put a second ball a few inches behind your club as you practice on the driving range. Brush the second ball back on your backswing as a reminder to keep the club low going back, and to come straight back before it sweeps through. This shot will come in time. Remember to throw caution to the wind and swing decisively to two. A good miss may go nearly as far as a perfectly struck shot if there is plenty of speed in the swing. The scorecard never asks for a tally of how many shots got in the air.

Wood or iron?

Choose to play a fairway wood only with a good lie. A good lie is level in the fairway and has a nice cushion of grass beneath the ball. There is the old joke about the player studying his fairway wood shot. "What's he waiting for?" one golfer asks another. "For more grass to grow under his ball." *Ba-bum.*

Under less than ideal conditions, an iron is always a better choice.

If you have any misgivings, opt for a 4- or 5-iron. Downhill shots are especially squirrelly. Choose a shorter, easier shot—i.e., get out of trouble—and count on a great chip, pitch, or putt to make up the difference. The same strategy applies to fairway bunkers. With the ball sitting down, even a little, into the sand, it's difficult for a larger clubhead to swing through. Hitting off of dirt, often called "hardpan," with little or no grass, same deal: choose an iron. The wood often hits the ground and bounces into the ball, resulting in a topped shot. In thick rough, choose a 5-iron and make an easier shot out of it.

Checklist

Have the hands just inside the left thigh.

Swing back low and slow until the shoulders stop turning.

Clip the tee or sweep the grass out from under the ball as you . . .

Decisively swing through to the finish.

Last word

This chapter's devoted to distance, but I want to leave you with one more piece of Harvey wisdom that has absolutely nothing to do with hitting the woods and everything to do with improving.

Harvey used to say that if you could get to the edge of the green in two and it took you three more shots to get the ball in the cup, it was like whiffing off the tee. A shot has been thrown away, essentially, regardless of how wonderful your drive. Of course, he was right. The advice underscores the importance of the short game.

HOW TO PRACTICE

The three clubs most often used are the putter, the wedge, and whatever club is used to tee off. Putter, wedge, 3-wood. Practice accordingly around these three clubs. Banging woods isn't the best use of time. We'll quickly tire and start making tired swings, too long and too fast.

Warm up by swinging at a single tee. Play a game. If you can sweep the tee out, put a ball on top. If you don't clip the tee or hit a poor shot, go back to sweeping the tee until you cleanly clip it. Sweep tees out in the yard. Remind yourself to finish the swing, getting all the way to "two."

After six or eight balls, trade the club out. Practice with the shorter clubs, the clubs that get the ball on the green—the 7-, 8-, or 9-irons. Hit a few of these and a few woods. Continue alternating. Pretend you're playing the golf course, hitting a wood off a tee, then a 5-iron off the ground, then a wedge. With the shorter clubs, really feel the swing in building consistency and familiarity.

To quell first-tee jitters, take a dry run by sticking a tee in the ground and sweeping it towards the fairway.

To get comfortable playing a ball off the ground, start by chipping the ball out on the range about thirty yards with your 3- or 5-wood. Shorten your backswing, step on the gas, and sweep the grass out from under the ball. Don't worry about it getting airborne. Think of a chip shot, as Harvey did, as a short drive. Simulate the chip swing, gradually increasing the length, and you'll be able to hit this shot.

Bunker Shots: Among the Shifting Sands

I'm in a greenside bunker.
I'm in a fairway bunker.
Get me outta here!

Golf began by the ocean on the sandy linksland that bridges the mainland and the sea. Here rabbits and grazing sheep made their home. To shield themselves from the harsh sea winds, the animals burrowed and nestled into the loamy soil. In time, grass worn or eaten away exposed the sand just beneath it.

These patches formed ideal natural tests for the golfer. Nothing's changed over the centuries in that respect. Today, course architects design bunkers using more scientific means, but the result is the same: strategically-placed pitfalls.

Harvey felt that if you dropped twenty-five balls into a bunker and couldn't leave until all the balls were out, eventually you'd realize that sweeping the sand from under each ball was the only way out. That may be a more punitive approach than I'd recommend these days, but it does prove a point. Kids often follow this pattern of learning and are pretty successful. After a time they solve the riddle.

Being proper

A *bunker* is the proper name for what most of us call a sand trap. The more venerable Scottish courses refer to them by name; the Church Pew and the Principal's Nose are two famous examples. Whatever they're called, these hazards can strike fear in the uninitiated.

The instruction for sand play has picked up on this, if I may say so, needlessly fueling anxieties. Maybe you've noticed that pros and instructors casually emphasize the ease of sand shots. Students hear this and no doubt stomach a sense of inadequacy when the shot doesn't come off so easily.

It's an unfair comparison, matching up with those who make golf their livelihood and habitually practice the shot during normal business hours. It reminds me of the professor who announced that the concept he was introducing was so simple a kindergarten student could get it on first hearing. That left students with a deep sense of foreboding. You may feel the same way about bunker shots.

The fear in the shot stems from the consequences. It's embarrassing to swing and have the ball stand its ground, or worse, force one's playing partners to seek cover from a speeding projectile. I've often thought the fear is similar to the fear of flying. It's not the flying that scares us, it's the prospect of falling 30,000 feet.

With proper technique and practice, like anything else, sand play becomes easier and less terrifying over time. And, in fairness to my colleagues, by saying something is not as hard as it looks, they're merely trying to put students at ease.

The bottom line
We have only one goal when our ball lands in a bunker: getting it out.

Putt it out

Long known as the "Texas Wedge," putting out of a bunker is an excellent option when the trap lacks a steep, overhanging edge or lip.

First, find a "highway" (the path to the hole) out. Use the same stroke as on the green. Take that same slow path away from the ball—one—and swing through—two—just like all the other strokes.

Look down the highway. Paint a line to the target. Leave the ball slowly and putt through to the other side. One. Two. How hard to hit it depends on the consistency of the sand, the distance to the hole, the rough and fringe around the green, etc. It takes a deft touch to get the ball close to the hole but using a putter, under the right conditions, works splendidly from a shallow-faced bunker. The old rule of thumb holds: If you can putt, do so. There's certainly no stigma attached to using a putter in the sand. The pros recognized the shot's reliability decades ago and don't hesitate to choose the putter as a creative and safe means of escape.

Look, putt, but don't touch

There is a bunker rule to remember, not of thumb but of play. In a bunker touching the sand with our putter, our club, our hand—anything—before we play is not permitted. That means no practice swings are allowed that disturb, or test, the sand in any way. It also means we have to be careful taking the club back, especially the putter, which we always take back low to the ground on our backswing. Touching the sand, except on the forward swing, is a two-stroke penalty.

Chip it out

Chipping from a bunker works best when the ball lies in a shallow trap, or rests along the upslope, sitting up cleanly. Stand close to the ball and think of the clubface as a putter. Set up as you would for a typical chip shot. The ball will be back slightly in the stance, the hands leaning towards the green. The club must come straight back and go straight through. As long as it stays on that path not much can go wrong. If the club catches too much sand, however, it will cause the club to turn and the ball to veer off target.

In considering this shot, be aware of the distraction the sand presents. A bunker is as much a mental as a physical hazard. Sand play often psyches out golfers. It makes us slow down or stop our swings going into the ball, the opposite of what we want to do—which is, of course, to step on the gas.

Driving a car through sand we'd certainly maintain our speed, or the tires might lose their traction and we'd get stuck. Same thing in a bunker. Keep the momentum going by picking up speed. **Step on the gas.**

Hit the big target

Mark Steinbauer, a friend and innovative instructor in Houston, uses the following approach with deep bunker play. The thinking reminds me of the old saying about the difference between the optimist and the pessimist. The optimist sees the doughnut, the pessimist sees the hole.

Preparing to play the shot, Mark suggests looking at the bunker as one big target. If he asked us to step into the bunker and hit the sand with our club, we could do that. With our eyes closed. With that objective anyone can hit the sand.

That's right, and that's why we should think of it simply as a large target with the ball as a smaller target. We are not going to swing at the little, bitty target. No, we are always going to swing at the big target, the sand, the one we can't possibly miss. **Forget about the ball. Think only of the sand. The secret to getting out of a bunker is decisively cutting a shallow swath of sand out from under the ball.**

Another popular visualization is to imagine the ball lying on a small island about six inches long. All six inches need to get out of the bunker with your shot. Leave the ball slowly and sweep quickly to the other side. Sweep the island out of the trap.

I didn't mention what club to use, but you'll have already gathered the sand wedge is the ticket. If you don't have one, check the equipment chapter. Every golfer should have one.

Greenside bunkers   **BALL POSITION AND STANCE**

Of the several keys to successful bunker shots, the consensus is that the ball should be up by the front foot. This makes getting the ball airborne easier. **Hands will be closer to the middle of the stance,** even with the zipper, rather than ahead of it as with other shots.

Your weight should be well forward, and it needs to stay there during the swing. Feel like you're leaning into a stiff wind. Hold that position throughout the shot. There's no weight shift and no turn; the weight starts on the left foot and stays there. It helps to dig in the feet to avoid the possibility of slipping. Also, keep the hands in close to the body as you would in preparing to hit a pitch shot.

There is a wonderful incongruity about sand play. One of the golf magazines describes it by noting that what doesn't work in the full swing works beautifully in the sand-shot swing. It's true. For instance, we use our arms in this shot, that's it. The sand swing is all arms. For another, we won't shift our weight during the swing. And, as we've seen, this is the one shot where we deliberately miss the ball and sweep the sand instead

Open clubface sand wedge

Line up a little to the left of the flagstick (about three feet). It's thought to offer a better look at the green. Pretend the hole has taken a step to the side. That spot now becomes the target. *Open* the clubface just a tad and grip the club. Dig in with your feet. Aim the leading edge of the club towards the flagstick. Swinging with just the arms, sweep a shallow swath of sand out of the trap. It needs to be shallow because the deeper into the sand the club digs, the more difficult it is to move. Start that swath behind the ball.

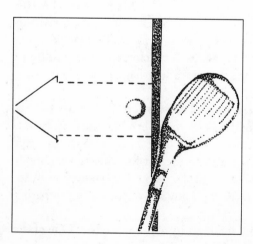

Open the 'toe' of the clubface to the right.

Finish strong!

Because we're in trouble—as when pressured or anxious to hit the ball a long way—there's a tendency to reach back too far. The farther back we swing, the longer the road to the other side. Home is in the follow-through position and we don't want to stray so far that we can't get there. Other than sweeping out the swath of sand, the most important part of this shot is making a decisive follow-through.

A quick tip on the grip **SAND SHOT GRIP**

Harvey suggested squeezing with the little finger and ring finger of the left hand to stabilize the club. This will keep the club in position on the way through and prevent twisting in the sand.

The shot will feel like you are throwing a ball underhand onto the green in a spray of sand.

A swing through the islands

Here's a tip to get in the habit of hitting the sand behind the ball, which is a contradiction of everything we've discussed. In golf, or any other game played with a ball and a stick, the objective is always to hit the ball. The only exception is when our ball lies in a bunker.

Imagine a small tee is underneath the ball. Clip the tee. Those balls that come out like rockets have been hit squarely. The club has missed the sand completely. Focus on the sand, the big target. It might even help to look a few inches behind the ball rather than right at it. Forget about words like *blast, dig, explode.* Think instead of cutting a shallow swath through the sand, or nipping the tee, or sweeping the sand onto the green. Whichever works best.

Getting ready to play out of a greenside bunker, this ball is closer to the right foot and the hands are behind it.

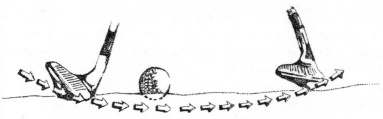

The sand is the big target. Sweep it out.

Fairway bunkers **BALL POSITION AND STANCE**

Bunkers away from the green are known as fairway bunkers. To play out of one, hit the ball, not the sand. Since the more sand we take the less distance we'll get, we want to catch the ball cleanly. The swing for this shot is more of an arm swing, without a normal turn or weight shift. The weight is more evenly distributed on both feet, as it would be on a normal fairway shot. We also don't dig in quite as much as when the sand is our target in a greenside bunker. The stance should still be secure to avoid sliding or slipping. Ball position with an iron is in the middle of your stance. It's possible to hit a wood out of a bunker in a shallow fairway trap. Use a 5-or 7-wood and play the ball closer to the left heel.

Take whatever club is certain to get you back on grass, either the sand wedge or 9-iron. Emphasize a shorter backswing and less movement below the waist. In golf talk this is referred to as keeping the lower half "quiet" during the swing. It's another way of describing an arm swing. Swing through and stay with the shot to the finish. **Take as little sand as possible.**

Buried alive?

A ball buried in the sand doesn't allow us to follow through as we would with other sand shots. Here's a shot that works well in those seemingly dire situations when the ball is "plugged" on the upslope of a bunker, or right under the overhang or lip. It's a fun shot and works like a charm. It'll look weird, but turn the pitching wedge towards your body so the face is *closed,* or hooded. (Yes, *pitching* wedge.) Okay, now just dig your feet in and swing as hard as you can. There won't be any follow-through, because the club will dig into the sand and stop. That's fine. The moment the club meets the sand it rights itself, and the ball pops out as pretty as you please.

Discretion

A last word on bunkers, fairway or greenside, steep-faced or shallow. There are times when our eyes get bigger than our stomachs and we're tempted to try too ambitious a shot. It reminds me of the Open, which is always played on the venerable links of the British Isles. The bunkers on those ancient courses can be treacherous. There are times when even the best players in the world recognize that discretion is the better part of valor. They play out to the side or even backwards. With experience they've learned that a low-percentage shot is simply not worth the risk. They take their lumps, get out safely, and then try and make up the stroke on the green. Better safe than sorry. Remember, when we land in a bunker we don't want to be greedy. We only want to get out. Choose the club that will be certain to do so, even at the expense of sacrificing distance.

Checklist

Here are the keys to consistently extricating yourself from a greenside bunker:

Play the ball off your left heel.

Have the grip point to the belt buckle.

Line up just a little to the left (about a foot) of your target.
"Open" the clubface (just a tad).
Hold on tight with the little and ring fingers of the left hand.
Lean on the left foot and keep the weight there.
Swing just with the arms.
Sweep a shallow swath of sand out of the bunker.

Fairway bunker checklist

Choose a club you know will carry over the edge of the trap.
Play the ball in the center of your stance with an iron, and
toward the front of your stance with a wood.
Take a slow and shorter backswing, and swing more with the
arms and hands.
Swing to the finish.

HOW TO PRACTICE

Familiarity and experience make all the difference in bunker play.
No surprise there. A distinct shot from the others we've learned,
it's not played off grass or a tee. With practice, bunker shots lose
their powers of intimidation.

There will always be a little doubt and uncertainty. Without
the threat of slowing play or embarrassment, a little quiet practice
instills the method with plenty of time for trial and error. Hopefully, it's not a shot we hit too frequently, but whatever time can
be devoted to it is time well spent.

Get in and practice sweeping some sand out—without a ball.

Then put a tee all the way down, into the sand, and clip it out. With that down, put a ball on a tee and clip them both out of the sand. When you can consistently spray sand and get away from the notion of hitting the ball, the shot will become almost as easy as instructors believe.

Trouble Shots:
Finding the Fairway from the Trees

I need to get back into play.
What if I can't get there from here?
Are trees really ninety percent air?

Back to the fairway. That's the goal when we find ourselves taking the scenic route through the woods. Get out of trouble and back into play.

Better players are masters of the positive spin, stoically dealing with adversity. They know the bounces in golf have a way of evening out. Rather than grumble over a difficult circumstance, successful golfers look upon tough shots as a test and an opportunity. It's a good attitude. After all, golfers have no one to blame for their misfortune but themselves.

Golf is always going to throw us something new, shots we never practice or never thought we'd need. Adjustment is a given in golf, and unpredictability part of the game's fascination. Conditions can change dramatically during the course of a round, and so can our luck and our swings.

Japanese restaurant menus note the more exotic pieces of sushi as "challenging." Likewise, the so-called trouble shots provide us with a greater measure of satisfaction when we can meet the challenge, extricating ourselves from a ticklish situation.

Faced with an unfamiliar shot, **slow down the backswing** and make everything more compact with less leg movement. Take a shorter length swing. **Concentrate on clipping whatever lies under the ball.**

When in doubt, settle on the surest escape route. Ask yourself: "What's the easiest way out?" The answer could mean swallowing some pride and sacrificing a stroke, making no progress at all towards the green. In thick grass, we may play out sideways, taking the path of least resistance. The safe play is akin to, in chess, moving a bishop out of danger to set up a later attack.

Deep, thick grass

Here's how to handle a ball in deep grass: The thicker the grass, the shorter the club. By shorter, I mean those with more loft, the 8- or 9-irons, pitching wedge, and sand wedge. The ball won't go as far, but these clubs will get you out of harm's way. Play the ball back in your stance, closer to your right foot. We're sacrificing distance, but the higher-lofted clubs are safer bets, more reliable in catching the ball and popping it out. Firmly grip the club. Because the grass will offer so much resistance, hold on tight. This is one shot where strong arm muscles clearly help.

Thicker grass than the fairway

A ball that is not in the real thick stuff requires a judgment call. With a ball that's easily seen, not *sitting down* in the grass, a 7-wood is a good choice. Make it shorter by holding the club lower down (leave about two inches of grip showing at the top), and swing away. The so-called "utility woods" are also designed for this shot and can be used in the same way.

Tall grass behind the ball

What to do when the grass interferes with taking the club back? This can happen in the fairway with a ball lying alongside the rough or in the fringe by the green. In either case, the higher grass prevents sweeping the putter or the club back from the ball as low as we'd like.

Play both shots as if in a bunker. Remember, we're not allowed to ground a club in a bunker, that is, we can't set it on the ground behind the ball. In this case, hold the club above the grass. Sweep it back slowly through the air, then take your normal swing.

In the dew

Treat wet fairways as if playing into the wind. Take *more* club (a 6-iron, for instance, instead of a 7-iron). Moisture severely impedes a ball's roll.

Ball in a divot

A similar prescription here. Play the ball towards the back of the stance. Close (hood) the club just a tad. **Shorter clubs are always easier to hit, and a better choice, when facing unfamiliar shots.**

Off dirt

Again, with a ball on dirt, play the ball closer to your right foot. Choose a 7-wood or a 5-iron, a club that instills confidence. Take the club back s-l-o-w-l-y.

Uphill and downhill lies

Not many driving ranges offer the opportunity to practice these tough shots. **The trick is to play the ball by the high foot with the weight on the low foot.** Stand so your shoulders slant, or follow, along the slope.

It's easier to do on uphill shots, but it's just as necessary to veer the shoulders down the slope for downhill shots. The less body movement during the actual swing the better. A shorter, more compact backswing, and less leg movement will help. Practice the swing a few times sweeping the club. Notice where it clips the grass. That will tell you where to play the ball. Again, a shorter club will make this shot easier, an 8- or 7-iron. As confidence increases on these shots, so can the length of the club used.

Ball below your feet

It's difficult enough to clip the grass when the ball is on level ground but when it's on a hill below the feet we have to adjust, bending down even further. *Really* flex those knees. Hold onto the end of the club, use just the arms with a shorter swing, as in a bunker shot. The knees stay flexed throughout the swing. **Straightening up will completely spoil any chance for a good shot.** There is a tendency to stand up at the end of this shot; be sure the ball is gone before you do.

Ball above your feet

With the ball closer to the body, this shot should be easier. Grip down lower on the club, making it shorter, and, again, keep the swing short and compact. **On all these trouble shots, remember to clip the grass beneath the ball.** Anxious to see the result, we often forget and stand up.

Bunker downhill

Consider coming out to the side. Play the ball in the middle of your stance. Shoulders should be slanted downhill, parallel to the slope. Grip way down on the club, with as much as three or four inches showing, and swing on through. Here's hoping you don't have too many of these.

Ball in the water

If you have to wade in, forget it. It is possible, however, to advance a ball providing it is only partially submerged. You want challenging? This is bungee-jumping challenging, but what the heck? It might only happen once every five years, but if you've got a change of clothes handy, pull out a pitching wedge and give it a go. Here are your marching orders: Play the ball back in the stance, hold on tight, damn the torpedos, and swing away! (It might be fun if someone has a camera, or at least a towel.)

Out of the woods

This shot comes in very handy. With a little imagination, it can be honed with practice. First find an opening. Play the ball back in your stance. (By now this should sound familiar.) Turn the club in, hooding it slightly. The best choices are the medium irons, preferably the 4-, 5-, or 6-irons.

This is one shot where we don't want the ball to go up in the air. Our aim instead is to thread it low through the trees and get out of jail taking the low road.

We've stressed throughout the book that following through is imperative to a good swing, making sure we finish, getting all the way to two. And so it is. For the moment, however, hold that thought. This Houdini-like escape from the trees is the one time when we purposely rein in our swings. Stop well before two. The follow-through on this shot is only about waist high. No higher.

To get the ball airborne we normally want that high follow-through. But not now, and not here, where we can't find the fairway from the forest. I can guarantee you one thing. That one time when you're trying to keep the ball low, you'll end up taking a full swing and hit the perfect shot—for the fairway—only to watch it soar briefly into the limbs before dropping a few yards ahead. To prevent this perfect, but inappropriate, shot—or rather, to delay it until it can do us some good in the fairway—stop the swing. Throw the child out of the porch swing. Stop at one and a half.

Look on the bright side. If you've been having trouble with the full swing, particularly in getting all the way to two, you already have this shot down.

Ninety percent air

Better golfers can *work* the ball, manipulating its flight like a good billiards player bends the cue ball around the eight ball. When you find yourself directly behind a tree or otherwise need to curve it left or right, turn the clubface in to make the ball go left (hook), or open it a little to make a shot go right (slice). Otherwise the swing should stay the same.

Pine straw and leaves

It's easy to inadvertently dislodge a ball in pine duff, so be careful placing a club behind the ball, especially in taking a practice swing. To hit this shot, the ball is back in the stance. Take a slow, compact backswing. Watch your footing. Because of the loose needles, a secure stance is a must. The same checklist applies in playing a ball off of a pile of leaves.

Simmer to boil

Not to dwell on it, but pressure necessitates a review in considering those infrequent shots that apply a little more twinge to the nerves. Of course, pressure is self-induced. Let's see . . . there's playing in the wind pressure, being pressed by the golfers from behind pressure, playing with client pressure, intimidation from hazards pressure, playing with better players pressure, playing with slower players pressure. And that's just a short list. I haven't even mentioned husbands, boyfriends, blind dates, or fathers. Your mileage may vary. Just know that pressure changes swings and tightens muscles.

We've been through this before, and we'll encounter it again. To combat tension, remind yourself to take . . . the . . . club . . . back . . . slowly . . . as . . . it . . . leaves . . . the . . . ball—very slowly for the first six to ten inches. I know it's hard to believe, but the space the length of a ruler sets the tempo of the whole swing. Think of starting back slowly and relax.

HOW TO PRACTICE

Practicing trouble shots and practicing golf in general can have a therapeutic effect; for many golfers it provides benefits similar to contemplative recreational activities like yoga or meditation. Practice is good for you and it's relaxing. It's a fact that the brain can't think of anything else and competently strike a golf ball. If nothing else, practice frees the mind from the confines of daily life. I've had lobbyists and attorneys tell me that once they dis-

covered golf as a means of entertaining clients, they stopped feeling obligated to go out for late drinks and dinner meetings.

Practice can be fifteen or thirty minutes. When I had small
children, I played tennis because it was a lot of exercise in a short
time. I asked Harvey once if tennis would hurt my golf, and he
said, "Well, it's just time away from golf." So instead of a set, I
started going out to the driving range. The freedom to fit practice
in on the run without needing a friend makes it ideal for anyone
pressed for time.

Ranges don't often offer the opportunity to practice trouble
shots, but there are two you can work on: hitting a ball out of a
divot and, with a little imagination, playing around trees.

Troublesome Shots

My swing has been possessed by demons.
Stop me before I shank/top/hit it fat again.
Why did the ball do that?

When your swing feels awkward and unfamiliar, start over with the grip. Next, review posture, aim, alignment, and ball position. The answers are in the fundamentals.

The irony is that when we're playing well we tend to take them for granted. But the more we play, the more lax we become. We start experimenting and guessing. Improvising makes us more vulnerable. One compensation leads to another and the door to advice opens. Soon we're disheartened, our faith and confidence shaken.

Then, the next time we play, we pay more attention to the basics, checking our grip and our stance, reminding ourselves to take aim and release tightness in our shoulders and elbows. Lo and behold, things are better. We're hitting the ball more solidly again.

Golf is a game of peaks and valleys. We'll never conquer it, but we need to prepare for the inevitable valleys. The overwhelming majority of problems with the swing can be traced to grip and stance. When a pattern of poor shots develops, something needs to be corrected. Then only through repetition and familiarity will the fundamentals become second nature.

A slice of life

Epic poems could be composed to the slice. While the oral tradition is undoubtedly ancient, the mountain of written instructional material pertaining to it dates to the late seventeenth century. The ball that circles off to the right saps distance and has a knack for getting lost. There are cures, thankfully, for this common cold of golf faults.

First, *strengthen* the grip, making sure the left hand is on top of the club, and that it hasn't slipped to the left (with the thumb on top). We're talking about a difference of less than an inch. **The left thumb should rest on the side of the grip and, looking down, you should see three knuckles of the left hand.** The line that forms between the thumb and index finger ideally points to the right shoulder.

Second, check tension. A death grip tenses the shoulders and the elbows, preventing the club from swinging smoothly. Open the floodgates. Release tension from the hands.

Third, check the shoulders. Be sure the clubface and shoulders are aimed the same way. Be advised that what seems logical with many swing fixes is often the opposite of the needed cure. This can take some getting used to. For example, the more one aims to the left to allow for a slice, the bigger the slice. **Work with a 7-iron until the slice is cured before moving on to longer clubs. Practice with the ball on a tee.**

My favorite cure

My favorite slice cure is detailed in the accompanying illustration. Set up four balls. Make sure one ball is placed directly behind the ball you're going to hit off a tee. Follow the path of the arrows in swinging and avoid hitting the balls. *Forget about the balls on the backswing.* Your only thought is following the

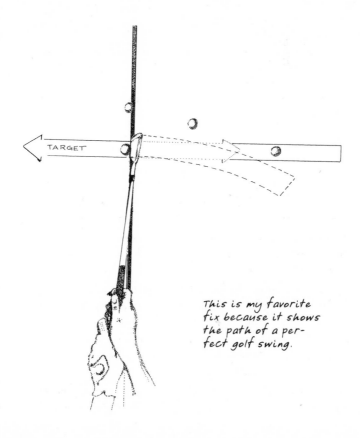

TARGET

This is my favorite fix because it shows the path of a perfect golf swing.

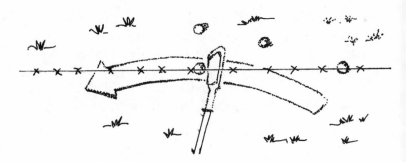

You can take this thought to the golf course and imagine your ball is under a fence.

curved line coming into the ball as you clip the tee. Look down until the tee has been clipped.

Fenced in

Another visualization is to imagine your ball under a fence about six inches high. Your job is to sweep the ball out from under it without catching the club on the fence. Work with a shorter club first, no more than a 7-iron. Be sure the swing goes under the fence before you look up.

Hitting the fence with the club would indicate a swing that produces a slice. You might think of this swing as "coming over the top" of the fence. Watch golf on television and you'll inevitably hear announcers describe someone's swing as "over the top," a common problem.

If the fence image doesn't do it for you, use the two-by-four plank that often divides many hitting areas at driving ranges. It's an excellent training aid. Place your ball a couple of inches away from the plank and hit your golf shot. Avoid hitting the plank. The prospect may be too daunting for some. Instead, take an

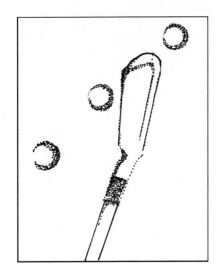

This drill makes you swing straight through the ball without detouring right or left.

empty shoe box to the range and place the ball two or three inches away from it. The slice swing will pop that shoe box and probably send it flying but, eventually, when you can hit a ball without hitting the box, your slice will be cured.

If none of the above helps your slice, take a lesson. Remember, a ball that *fades*—the better-behaved cousin of the slice which starts out straight and finishes slightly to the right—is perfectly acceptable.

The three balls

Here's another cure. Line up three balls diagonally (see illustration), about two inches apart. The object is to hit *only* the middle ball. Two or three balls may be inadvertently hit, but this is practice. No one cares. Everyone on the range is too busy working on their own swings to notice.

A slice swing can catch all three balls. This is, again, hitting "over the top." Concentrating on that middle ball will keep your focus on sweeping straight through and cure that slice.

The Pull

A close relative of the slice, a *pulled* shot starts left and stays left. The cure for it is similar to slice fixes. Go back and feel that full-swing stretch. The antidote is to be sure to complete the shoulder turn and to sweep the ball out from under the fence. The three-ball drill will also help.

Peek at the clubface. Aimed a little left? Ask a friend to stand behind you and check your aim. Line the club up more precisely. You're not asking your friend for a lesson, only for a second opinion on aim and alignment.

Hooking

Everyone wants this problem until they have it. The *hook* is an overgrown *draw*, which is in itself very desirable. A "draw" is a ball that curls in flight in a controlled arc from right to left. Too much of it, however, leads to a hook, the ball that flies uncontrollably left. As "hookers" know, the rough is as deep on the left as it is on the right.

The correction is to *weaken* the grip. Experiment first with the right hand, then with the left. Make the tees (held between your fingers) point to the chin. One dose of medicine won't work overnight. A chronic hook can take such pains to eliminate that it nearly short-circuited the great Ben Hogan's career.

If changing the grip doesn't help, invest in a lesson from an experienced teacher. Remember, a ball that draws a little to the left is what we all want. Once it hits the ground, a draw gets lots of extra roll.

The push

A *pushed* shot starts out right of the target and stays that way. It doesn't allow us a moment of hope by going straight and then turning right, like a slice. The cure is to check the clubface, aim straight, and try to hit the ball twenty yards to the left. It sounds harder than it is. Think of a large tree directly in front of you with a pond to the right. You *have* to miss that tree and the water by aiming at the pond and making that ball go left. Now, should the ball start going twenty yards left on every shot, you've thought about it enough. Forget about it on your shots and you should start hitting the ball straight again.

Topping

To cure a spate of topped shots, imagine entering a room with a very low ceiling. You can't stand up. At the end of the swing, you're still leaning over. Another thought is to pretend your head is against a wall. Swing and take a normal turn, but the head has to stay touching the wall.

Picture being behind a tall tree you can't possibly hit a ball over. Try to hit the ball under the limbs instead. Harvey suggested visualizing a table a few feet out in front of us and imagining hitting the ball under the table.

Last word on topping: keep the knees flexed. Straightening them during the swing encourages a topped shot.

Chunky

Hitting behind the ball, also known as hitting it *fat,* can so thoroughly rattle a golfer that it causes a repeat performance. Slowing down and extreme caution are what does it. Keeping the weight on the right foot throughout the swing will also make it happen. Perhaps the most common cause is picking up the club (as if preparing to hammer a nail) rather than sweeping, low and slow.

The cure is to step on the gas. Once you reach the top of the backswing, make sure to swing through to two. The clubhead should be traveling at its fastest speed well past the ball, not before it gets there. A good shot would have a count of one back, two through. A fat shot would have a count of one back, two down to the ball (*whump,* tulip planting-sized divot) and three, finally, at the finish, if it makes it.

The sh-h-h-ank

Jarring to pronounce, horrid to watch, the *shank* is an affliction that daunts even the very best players. Harvey wouldn't use the word. He called them lateral shots. Thankfully, to cure the sh-h-an-, uh, lateral, doesn't require a trip to the Mayo Clinic.

Often when shots go "dead right," the ball hits the heel, where the shaft attaches to the club, and spins off sideways. There is a bright side to a shank, if you can believe it. A lateral is very close to being a good shot. The ball is almost hit in the center of the clubface, as it should be. Almost.

Here's how to cure it:

Place a tee two inches from a ball, side by side. Swing at the ball, miss the tee. Doing this will correct the fault without your having to think about it. If the problem persists, put something

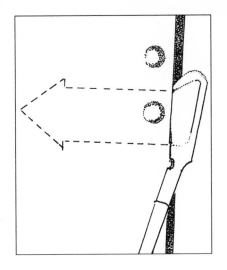

Hit that inside ball and that will cure the shank.

larger down to keep from hitting two things at once: an extra ball, a headcover. Believe me, this will cure a shank. On the course, address the ball on the toe of the club and tell yourself to hit the ball on the toe until the shank disappears.

An Equipment Primer

*I need to buy or upgrade golf clubs.
How much should I spend?
Who has the best selection of rubber iron covers in
    designer shades?*

Two subjects invariably come up at the end of every school: equipment and lessons. Potentially ticklish and increasingly costly, these rites of passage ultimately help us decide whether golf is worth our time and expense.

Women need to be particularly attentive to equipment, because for years many of us have been inappropriately fitted or sold clubs we didn't need. With clubs and, to a lesser extent, instruction, golf is big business. The menus are crowded with products and services overheated by competition, technology, and, let's face it, hype. Until *Consumer Reports* gets around to it, let me try and sort out the gray areas that typically give golfers, particularly women, the biggest headaches.

Buying a better game

You've probably heard this one: "Wait until you learn how to play before buying decent clubs." No one wants to shell out big bucks without being certain of their commitment, obviously. Golf clubs aren't cheap. But it's penny-wise and pound-foolish. A new tennis player wouldn't be expected to start out with a beat-up racket missing a few strings, just as an aspiring runner wouldn't take to the streets in sandals before progressing to a quality pair of running shoes.

New and expensive equipment isn't mandatory, however. There is an abundance of reliable, commendable—and affordably priced—used equipment. Like other consumer goods, golf clubs turn over seasonally. The quest for new models that promise (and even occasionally deliver) more distance, better control, more of this and less of that, never ends. The marketplace creates a bountiful supply of quality used clubs. If a bargain isn't of paramount concern, go ahead and get a top of the line set. Although some depreciation can be expected, you won't lose as much money sticking with name-brand equipment. In that respect, golf clubs are like automobiles. The more paid up front, the better the return in trade.

Beyond price, and irrespective of brand, there are benchmarks to keep in mind before pulling out a credit card. For many years women were notoriously slighted with clubs, a situation that seems to be improving almost daily.

One size doesn't fit all

Those under 5'5" are looking at standard ladies equipment; those taller will need longer clubs. For some reason, women's clubs have traditionally been designed for shorter women, and thus are shorter in length. **A woman 5'9" cannot swing the**

same club a woman 5'2" swings. There's more misinformation and confusion over club length than just about anything else. A club that's too short limits the arc that generates acceleration and gives us distance. A longer club can always be gripped down an inch or two. I'll never forget a couple who came to me for lessons. She was about 5'10", he was several inches shorter. Her clubs were too short and his were too long. I suggested they switch. Women beware. Don't start the game on the short end of the stick.

Clubs are now routinely tailored to the golfer based on several measurements, including arm length. Many golf shops see a woman walk through the doors, however, and immediately steer her over to the shorter "ladies' line" clubs. The other misfortune I often see is ill-fitted clubs given as gifts. When a man walks into a store to purchase clubs for a woman, frequently no consideration is given to her size. Clubs need to fit like skis or any other piece of personalized sports equipment. Somehow this misinformation about women's club lengths has been perpetuated over the years from club maker to distributor to pro shop and golf store.

It's interesting to note that equipment geared for seniors is always longer, the theory being that as we get older the extra length will provide more distance. Women need distance from the beginning.

Part of the confusion likely results from the evolution of club sales. Not that long ago, clubs were almost exclusively sold in pro shops and the occasional department store. The market has dramatically changed. Courses have now all but conceded club sales to golf-specific stores, among them several highly competitive chains. Pro shops no longer offer the selection or price and subsequently rely less on clubs as profit centers. At the same time, the used club market has blossomed. And women's-specific golf stores, like Empowered Women's Golf, are carving out a niche by better meeting their growing clientele's needs. That's not to say there aren't exceptions. Many pro shops still sell clubs. But in the same way office products, to pick one category, have seen the growth of superstores, golf equipment seems to have gone down a similar road.

Shafts

The golf club's shaft is the most important factor to consider in purchasing clubs. The shaft provides the whipping motion during the swing that drives the ball. Regardless of what material is used, flexibility is the key. *Flex* can run the gamut from very stiff to very flexible. The more flexible the shaft, the less effort required to hit the ball; in other words, the more flexible the shaft, the greater the action. Flexible shafts are standard with women's clubs. Tall women, however, should buy men's clubs which, for them, are the proper length—and they should have senior (more flexible) shafts, or those marked "light" flex. To add to the confusion, manufacturers use different names to identify various grades of flexibility. Flexible is usually labeled "L" for ladies; "A" flex, or light flex, is appropriate for seniors and tall women.

Irons

Sets typically include a 3-iron through pitching wedge. A 2-iron, sometimes available as an option, is unnecessary, and most players can do without a 3-iron. Marketing and technical jargon are unavoidable in purchasing clubs. Most of it can be thankfully discarded. The length of the club and the shaft's flex are the most important considerations. Try and hit some "demo" (short for demonstration) clubs. It's like buying a pair of shoes. Even if you're sure of your size you still wouldn't buy a pair without trying them on. The same is true with clubs. With the right flex and length in mind, try to hit several different brands. Even a newcomer will quickly get an idea of what she likes. A golfer can enter the game with a partial set consisting of a 3-, 5-, 7-, 9-iron, sand wedge, and putter.

Woods

Woods offer a similar assortment of high-tech design features. Many golfers, professionals included, prefer woods over long irons. Woods bring to bear more mass when swinging through the ball and, thus, generate more distance than irons. Many golfers trade out the 3-, 4-, and 5-irons for the 5-, 7-, and 9-woods, respectively. A set comprised of the 3-, 5-, 7-, and 9-woods with the 6-, 7-, 8-, 9-irons, pitching and sand wedges, and putter would be an ideal grouping. That adds up to eleven clubs; the legal limit is fourteen for tournament players. The fewer choices the better.

Woods do not have to match irons, and woods do not have to match each other. The pros often mix and match favorites. If you find one you like, put it in your bag.

One desirable addition is the utility wood, meant for tight spots and designed to get the ball into the air easier. A popular and venerable choice is a *baffler,* so named for the two rails that run along the bottom, or sole, of the club. This club also provides extra weight designed to sweep through thick grass and quickly get the ball aloft. These clubs are particularly handy on courses with narrow fairways and high rough.

Training wheels

Avoid starter sets. They call them that, I've always thought, knowing full well that no one will play with them for very long.

Cheaper, a poorer grade all around, they always include a driver which no novice needs. Pass on to quality used equipment or fitted component sets.

Made to order

Component clubs come in parts and are then assembled. Given the number of clubheads, shafts and grips, combinations are practically infinite. Club making has become a popular hobby for a lot of people who enjoy tinkering. Those who have moved beyond the hobby stage are professionally certified.

The myriad of available options allows the golfer to pick and choose components given their personal characteristics, tastes, and budget. It also affords the luxury of buying a few clubs at a time. Always try and buy the best quality components. Going this route you're already saving money, so why scrimp on quality?

Given the selection and the vagaries of the marketplace, it's wise to comparison shop. Golf clubs don't wear out. Better clubs are fashioned with the attention to detail found in any superior manufactured product. **"Pro line equipment" is the one phrase worth remembering.** It's rarely sold in department or discount stores. The brand name companies take considerable pains with respect to workmanship and research and development. You're paying for it, but it's worth it. Their quality controls ensure the clubs are properly graduated and balanced. How that translates to you is that you'll have better misses.

The club market changes so quickly it's difficult to keep up with technology. Like any changing market, whether it's computers, automobiles, or golf clubs, seek out a knowledgeable salesperson. Call golf stores or pro shops and ask for advice over the phone. The more information you gather, the more qualified you'll be to make your selection. Keep in mind that many women comfortably play with men's clubs, which are usually longer than clubs designed specifically for women.

While pro shops have lost much of their club sales margin to the chain stores, a pro is still an excellent resource in purchasing clubs. He or she may also be able to work with you on price. These days clubs are typically bought without a lot of information or expertise. Just about anything can be bought "off the rack," even over the Internet, with little guidance. Just know that, like shopping at outlet stores, buying clubs from golf discounters is not without its hazards. What is gained in price is typically lost in personal service and expertise.

My best advice is to shop around, as you would before making any major purchase. The increasing competition among club-makers has been a bonanza for the consumer. I recommend trying out clubs before buying them. Call and ask if the store has "demo" clubs that you can hit to help get an idea of what you like. Experiment with different sets and models, irons and woods, like taking a test drive before buying a car. An opinion usually forms in the mind's eye pretty quickly.

Sand wedge

You gotta have one. The sand wedge is specifically designed to get the ball out of sand, and it works superbly, as we've seen. The club actually slides underneath the ball and cuts through the sand without digging into it.

It's not only useful in bunkers but also from short distances from the rough and fairway. Like woods, wedges do not have to match a set of irons. That's one of the zillion options in assembling a set. Equipment companies renowned for their wedges are another indication, if any were needed, of how specialized a once fairly humble and modest enterprise has become.

Gap wedge

This club falls between a sand wedge and pitching wedge in how far it moves the ball. Those who can be precise in knowing how far they hit their clubs often find this wedge fills a gap, thus the name, in yardage. The club is for those situations when the green cannot be reached with a sand wedge, but a pitching wedge is *too much* club.

Lob wedge

This is another specialty wedge that goes even higher and shorter than a sand wedge. This is the club you'll often see the pros use to pull off some little bit of short game magic. It's almost like a trick shot. The lob wedge flops the ball out of thick grass almost straight up in the air. It's a useful club on courses that require short shots that must get up in a hurry, for instance, to carry a bunker and then stop quickly on the green. It is, however, a difficult club to hit and should be used by golfers who have the time to practice it.

Picking a putter

Choosing a putter boils down to personal preference, but like any of the other clubs—more so, really—it's advisable to test out a fair sampling and be sure before making your purchase. Aside from looks, the putter should be long enough not to cause back strain and short enough not to get hung up in your golf shirt during the stroke.

Golf balls

The operative word in the golf ball you should play is *round*. I'm not being glib. The quality of the manufacturing process today is so good that the likelihood is considerably higher that the ball will be lost long before it wears out.

There are basically two kinds of balls. The expensive ones are for players who hit the ball far enough and consistently enough, and for whom cutting into the softer material and cost aren't issues. For them the reputed softer feel and more optimal spin ratios may indeed result in better performance. These balls take their name from their balata cover, a substance that originates from the gum of the balata tree.

The majority of golfers will want to play with a ball that promises more distance and greater durability. These are also cheaper and have a Surlyn cover. The difference in price will be immediately noticeable. Balata will always appear somewhere on the packaging of the expensive balls.

Another recommended option are x-outs. These balls, typically for cosmetic reasons, did not meet the manufacturers' standards and can't, in good faith, be sold at full retail. They're seconds, basically. A number may have been smudged or the company name not printed perfectly. Logoed balls that end up as x-outs may simply have been the result of an overrun or a cancelled order. They are an excellent value.

Grips

Grips should be replaced when they feel slick. Slippery grips cause us to squeeze the club, which we know adds tension unnecessarily. (Same song, second verse.) This is a maintenance issue, akin to changing your car's tires or oil, except that no light flashes on the dashboard.

Here's how to be sure your grips are the right size: Grip the club, and the middle two fingers of your left hand should just touch your left palm.

Bags

A carry-on limit? In golf? Not exactly. Bags come in sizes (and tastes) that run the equivalent of a cosmetics bag to a sea trunk. If you're walking, weight is an obvious consideration. Numerous options abound, from tripod leg stands to backpacklike shoulder straps. Ask for or see that the bag comes with a rain hood.

Travelling with clubs is an issue. Aware that guests are not enthralled with lugging their golf clubs through airports, resorts are increasingly upgrading the selection and quality of rental clubs, an amenity ski resorts recognized years ago by providing quality skis, boots, poles, etc. There are numerous options in travel covers designed to protect clubs, from hard cases with rollers to soft-padded bags. To play with your own clubs away from home, you'll need one. Given the costs of a good set of clubs these days, not to mention the sentimental attachment, and the rough and tumble of baggage handlers, protecting one's investment with a sturdy cover seems prudent, at the very least.

Hand in glove

A golf glove falls under the optional category. They offer a surer grip. They're worn on the left hand but buy one for your right hand too, and your hands will be warm for cold weather golf.

What you don't need

Golf makes amends for its high standard of civility with a record number of endless doodads. No game has more "stuff" to encumber, bemuse, and fortify the devotee than golf. The sales of these products must be astronomical. I won't even get into relatively normal accessories: belts, sunglasses, hats, jewelry, etc.

Many of these things we can do without. Unless you're the white glove type, you don't need covers for your irons, whether of durable plastic or pliable Neoprene, with attachment strings or without. They just add ten more little things to leave around the course that you'll have to double back to retrieve. Tubes meant to protect the shafts are also unnecessary. They add weight to the bag and offer a needless source of frustration in trying to find the darn things to replace a club. The shafts might scar up a bit, but it's nothing that will impede their performance.

The innocent golfer should also beware of gimmickry in the form of swing aids that could easily, in another time, have been sold from the back of buckboards. If they attach to the body, they're not allowed on the golf course. Sad to say, the only path to better scores is practice and playing. Pitchmen still offer products that promise the moon and stars. All that's required is to call the 800 number on your screen and agree to three easy installments of $39.95. It has been noted that one of the pleasures golf affords is that when all else fails, there is always something new to buy, and golfers, male and female, can always go shopping.

CHAPTER
11

A Lesson Primer

What do I look for, and look out for?
What if I don't understand my instructor?
How do I deal with unsolicited advice, tips, etc.?

There was a time when I began looking around for a golf teacher to improve my game and save my marriage. My husband was my biggest fan; an excellent golfer, he was also my harshest critic. Things were taking a turn for the worse. Not only was my golf not improving, there were times when we left the golf course with Roane mad and me in tears.

Harvey then shared with me perhaps his most enduring bit of advice. The worst thing that could happen to a golfer, he said, would be to have the world's two best instructors. I should decide on only one. To my husband's credit, Roane was delighted with my choice. My golf improved and we're still married.

Golf has always been a sociable game. The free exchange of ideas is part of a general climate of amiability. The reason we love golf—and the reason it is such a wonderful game—is that it can be shared. Everyone pulls for one another. The same person imploring you to keep your head down and your eye on the ball

genuinely wants you to do well and feels an obligation (to a point) to help you through the inevitable frustration.

Good intentions run smack up against two realities. Those inspired with the desire to help others (it's nothing personal) fail to realize that what works for one golfer isn't always universal. Worse, like other quack cures, their advice can have the opposite effect. Harvey always said that no instruction was better than poor instruction. This brings to mind Tommy Armour, who frequently observed what he described as "the unknowing teaching the unsuspecting."

Thank the Samaritan for his interest, for taking time away from his golf to help yours. But whatever is said must go in one ear and out the other. "I'm going to the range tomorrow and I'll try it out then," or, "It's too much to think about now. Let's wait until after the round," should be sufficient to free yourself from the charlatan's clutches.

Those who teach

Every golf course has a head professional and a staff of assistants. Despite long hours and low pay, a steady stream of aspirants flock to golf. **You want to learn from someone who enjoys teaching and who teaches a lot.** Inquire as to how often a prospective instructor gives lessons. Ask about their golf experience, their playing accomplishments, where they learned the game, the teachers they admire or have read. Just an informal background check. Whether you've heard the names or not isn't important. You just want a sense that this is someone energetic and conscientious about the profession.

The more experience a teacher has, presumably the more he knows, and the better he'll be in sharing that understanding. Playing credentials are no guarantee of teaching competence. Think back on your best teachers and identify the appropriate attributes.

Golf is an inexhaustible subject. The learning process never stops, for teachers as much as for students. Instructors continually compare notes. They experiment and research, even take lessons from one another. Often I learn as much from a given lesson as the student does.

The most successful teachers find something to build upon in every student's swing. Experience has taught him or her what to recognize, and what to work on. Emphasizing the negative serves no productive purpose. Instructors are certainly aware of the faults, but they focus their student's attention on the positives without belaboring the obvious problems.

There are so many ways to say the same thing. If you're not making progress, ask the pro to rephrase the instruction, or use a more familiar analogy. You're the customer. This is for your benefit. You're learning the techniques, he already knows them. There are teachers who easily lapse into technical mumbo-jumbo and leave their students feeling confused, uncoordinated, slow, physically challenged.

For me, nothing brings this home like computers. Following an instructor breezing over the keyboard, showing the various functions, clicking things on and off the screen with ease, my eyes glazed over. I just couldn't get it. I finally traded out golf lessons with University of Texas computer professor, Glenn Downing, who spoke my language. He went along to buy my computer. I accompanied him club shopping. He never scolded me with, "No, no, no. Not that key. That's the 'delete' key." And I never chastised him with, "How many times do I have to show you that grip?" We discovered several things about teaching: that we often went back over ground we'd previously covered, and we were reminded of jargon's general pervasiveness. Those who talk the talk have a decided edge over those who don't. You want a golf instructor who's good at translation.

Three questions

A golf instructor needs to know three things:
1. **How long have you played?**
2. **How often do you play?**
3. **What's happening to your balls? (Are they slicing, hooking, topping, short—a combination?)**

Those surefire tips from your husband's half-brother? Keep them to yourself. Better yet, forget them.

All a doctor wants to know is what's wrong, what are the symptoms. The diagnosis is his business. You're paying for a thorough examination and, hopefully, a prescription for a cure. The experience should be similar with a golf instructor. Pros are used to hearing patients analyze their afflictions. Tommy Armour wryly noted, "The worst golfers are those that can identify their faults and come to a lesson wanting to know more of them." Simply providing the answers to the above questions speeds the process. The "symptoms" will make themselves apparent soon enough.

Women teaching women

I'm often asked whether women pros are better at teaching women. All of the great instructors that I have known or read about were gender-blind. I do think women respond better to stories and situations that are more familiar to them, but the same holds true for men. Women who feel intimidated by a male pro may want to seek out a female instructor. Male or female, what's most important is the teacher's ability to communicate.

It must be said: Ego is not unknown in golf teaching circles. There are those who take a paternal interest in a star pupil's triumphs, viewing the success as their own. And when the student falters? Naturally, the teacher's blameless.

We are always reading how so-and-so, famous teacher, helped so-and-so, pro golfer, win the tournament. But when the golfer falters we never seem to read those same plaudits. No one asks those playing poorly for the name of their teacher. This, of course, is indicative of a human weakness not exclusive to golf.

Good teachers often provide as much moral and emotional support to their students as technical instruction. The point is:

You should enjoy your lesson. It should be fun. Learning through fear and intimidation is a waste of time. If it's not working out, don't hesitate or worry about hurting anyone's feelings. Competent teachers won't mind your seeking advice from others if progress is at a standstill.

Take some crib notes

With a lesson still fresh, jot down a few notes before leaving. You'll be surprised how often you'll return to them. Twenty years later, those key points will still be valid. That's why instruction books stay in print for decades.

Group lessons

Not only are group lessons cheaper, there's safety in numbers—i.e., they offer a less intimidating setting, especially for newcomers. The give-and-take provides welcome learning opportunities. People ask questions beneficial to others. A group setting also provides a natural introduction to others with similar skills and a ready source of people to play with. Since we can't see ourselves, it's important to observe golfers of various sizes, ages, and individual styles. My students get actively involved with each other's progress by appraising grips and checking backswings. In the process, they're learning for themselves.

It shouldn't have to be said: New students should be treated as valued customers. It's simply good business sense. You are a potential source of revenue for clubs, green fees, cart rentals, range balls, corporate outings, food and beverages, etc., all of which positively and directly impact the pro's income and the course's bottom line. The sharper ones recognize a lesson as an opportunity to make a good impression. The pro who looks down on new golfers has a lot to learn about customer loyalty. He'd surely fail Business Sense 101. Beginning golfers are some of the most eager and appreciative students an instructor will ever have. All of the great teachers know this and all of them, to a man or woman, enjoy working with new golfers.

Golf schools

Intensive and fun, golf schools are a great escape. Golfers return home positively bristling with new information. Of course, one needn't be sequestered at a resort for three days to improve. If the time were similarly devoted at a local course, taking a lesson

every morning and practicing in the afternoons, strides would be made. But we're just not going to do that, and doesn't it sound more fun to go to Hilton Head or Maui?

A fellow instructor once put it to me that golf schools take a thirty-minute lesson and spread it out over three days. That's not necessarily such a bad thing, even if it were true, when we include down time spent on the beach or enjoying the spa. The positive side is the emphasis on fundamentals. The downside, of course, is the price. But sometimes we just need to get away, and if we look at it in that light—as a vacation and a chance to meet people and see new places—why not? Be forewarned: Golf schools will have you hitting a lot of balls and working fairly vigorously.

Swing tests

Videotaping has become an integral teaching tool, allowing us a detailed picture of our swings. There's no question that the footage is fun to see. It may be a difference between the sexes, but I've noticed that women tend to focus on the negatives of their swing and appearance. Employing the unblinking eye of the camera allows a teacher to break down a two-second swing into one hundred parts and positions and analyze each one. We can even compare ourselves through the magic of slow-motion replay with the top professionals. What's missing, of course, is what the camera can't show. The touring pros invest untold hours in their swings.

My own opinion is that the use of videotaping benefits the experienced player more than the newcomer. A popular teaching tool nonetheless, video will inflate the cost of the lesson. Just remember that no matter how good that swing looks on tape, it can't be bottled and taken to the course. And, looking on the bright side, what may not look good on tape may work great on the golf course. Lee Trevino once quipped that his swing was so unusual that if he'd seen it on tape he would never have pursued a professional career in golf.

CHAPTER
12

Frequently Asked Questions Answered

Can we talk?
Staying out of trouble.
Tell me about your good shots.

Pertinent questions often go unasked, particularly between a female golfer and her male instructor. Why? Because golfers are not so much shy, I think, as overly polite. Rather than broach a delicate subject, or ask for a better explanation, we prefer to suffer in silence. It's understandable, to a point: No one likes bringing attention to their blind spots. It's like men who'd rather keep driving around lost than stop to ask directions.

Here are a number of topics raised in golf schools over the years:

Q: Do breasts hamper the golf swing?
A: The truth is that a broad-shouldered man makes the same adjustments in swinging a golf club as a woman with a large bust and broad shoulders. Each has difficulty forming a traditional strong grip. This is the adjustment they both make: the left hand

should rest on top of the grip—in a weak position, granted—but (and this is important) their right hand remains on the club in the strong position we've discussed all along, with the crack pointing to the right shoulder.

The well-endowed woman needs to keep the elbows and shoulders relaxed to avoid an uncomfortable squeeze, but this is, again, nothing new. We've been discussing this all along for all golfers. Finally, there's no reason why women with large breasts and narrow shoulders can't hold the club with a strong grip and make a good shoulder turn.

At the risk of political correctness, I did read a funny, and accurate, description of the breasts during the golf swing. It is to "point them back and point them forward."

Q: I hit all my clubs the same distance. Why?

A: A frequent complaint of new golfers, the good news is that the shorter clubs can be hit quite well. The bad news is that the longer clubs are not hit as solidly—thus creating the problem. A strong grip, relaxation, a good shoulder turn, and clipping the grass or the tee out from under the ball should help. Of course, how far golfers hit their clubs differs from one player to the next. Men, for example, may average fifteen to twenty yards between clubs, and women ten to fifteen yards. Keep in mind the old adage that we "drive for show and putt for dough," and the practice of both will improve the score—and your distance. Re-read the distance sections in the woods and full swing chapters to review.

Q: What is course management?

A: Sensibly avoiding trouble on the golf course is, like so many other aspects of golf, easier said than done. Course designers specialize in using the natural setting to tweak the imagination. The good ones skillfully tempt the golfer with the deft use of artificial and natural hazards. Pull off the harder shot and reap the reward; miss it, however, and pay a price.

The better architects always leave an *out,* a safer, easier way around. Identifying and following it (also easier said than done) is course management. It's the prudent golfer who heeds Tom Kite's advice: "Know where to miss."

Here's an example of what I mean: With water in front of the green, choose the club that may be too much if you hit it perfectly, but will end up on the green even if you don't absolutely nail it. Anything to avoid the water.

Those who tend to slice should tee the ball up on the right side of the tee box and aim out to the left. This affords a larger potential landing area. Those prone to a hook should move over and tee up on the left hand side of the teeing ground.

Remember, when in trouble, getting out is the goal, even if it costs a stroke to get back to the fairway. Be your own best friend on the golf course. Encourage rather then berate, accentuate the positive. There is such a thing as a good miss in golf, a ball that doesn't look good getting there but that makes the fairway or the green all the same. Take them when you can get them. Appreciate them.

Q: Is there a perfect golf swing?

A: The perfect swing is described in technical terms as the club coming in low, slightly inside the target line, with the clubface aimed at the target. It also means that backswings can take many paths and detours. Some may be too long, others too short and entirely on the wrong road, but amazingly they end up where they need to be—coming squarely into the ball—at the precise moment of truth.

We're all different sizes and shapes, with varying degrees of coordination and flexibility. Some swings that are unconventional (okay, funky) work just fine—testament that there's more than one way of getting there. It's when swings don't arrive at the ball headed in the right direction and on the right path that instructors have to figure out how to get golfers back onto the main road.

Q: *What if I can't play or practice very much?*

A: For the amount of time you're able to get out on the golf course or practice, you may be a fabulous player. I mean that. Golf is unquestionably a lot easier without a career or a family, something overlooked all too often by those of us who teach golf.

Obviously, the pros find it much more convenient than the rest of us to go out and perfect their swings or their short games. Golf is their passion, but it's also their job. Not many of us can steal away that kind of time for a recreation, engrossing as golf can be.

The most popular book ever written (diet books follow cookbooks as perennial biggest sellers) may someday be a diet book entitled *Lose Twenty Pounds in Twenty Days and EAT ALL YOU WANT! GUARANTEED!* Its golf companion might be titled *Take Twenty Strokes off Your Game in Twenty Days WITH ABSOLUTELY NO PRACTICE!*

Despite Madison Avenue's best efforts, it's not going to happen. Still, we keep buying diet books that offer painless, effortless weight loss. And the golf-book-buying public can't get enough of quick cures that don't require any effort. Golf should be fun. If your goal is to be a tournament-level golfer, go for it. Work hard, put in the sweat equity, stay with it; the same goes for losing weight. But let's not forget the big picture. Golf is about enjoying the outdoors and our companions, and challenging ourselves in a fun way.

Q: What's the right age to start kids?

A: Harvey believed the age to begin golf is when the child shows an interest. Start with a putter and golf etiquette. A cut-down 7-iron, an adult club shortened to accommodate a child's grip and height, is where to start with the swing. Lessons are a good idea when the child asks for them. They won't need them often.

Davis Love III is a highly regarded and thoughtful touring pro who learned the game from his golfing father, a celebrated teacher. They remained the best of friends as "Trey" matured and grew as a player. In his book about his dad, a lovely remembrance called *Every Shot I Take,* Davis details one of the facets of their relationship that made it special. I've tried to follow the advice with one of my daughters, a ranked amateur until she had her baby. Davis wrote that his father never gave him advice unless he asked for it. As difficult as this is for a parent (or spouse, or friend), stay with it and the relationship will endure.

Q: Why is it that I can make a perfectly fine practice swing and then can't hit the ball?

A: Because practice swings aren't the identical swings we think they are. Clipping the grass or sweeping an exact spot under the ball serves to square the clubhead; in other words, it's orienting the clubface to hit a straight shot. Just swinging the club casually won't do that. Your practice swings should approximate the swing you want to make as closely as possible. Otherwise, don't take one. The backswing isn't nearly as important as the path the club takes through the ball to the swing's finish.

Q: Are college golf scholarships really out there?

A: A golf scholarship is one of the easiest of the athletic scholarships available to young women. Many go unfilled, and one third are annually given to foreign students. If you, or someone of your acquaintance, can consistently shoot scores in the eighties, the opportunity to receive a scholarship is a real possibility.

Q: How many practice swings should I take?

A: One is enough, and it's okay not to take any. More is just accumulated clutter. We know mechanical thoughts are devastating. They're like throwing sand into the gears of your swing. If you take two swings, which one do you use with the ball? On the golf course, get away from worrying about swing mechanics. Think about where you're going. Concentrate on the target. Step up, clip the tee, hit the target.

Speaking of practice swings, make sure in taking one that it's completed. All the way. I was in Harvey's living room once, talking with him about the golf swing. I casually picked up the club he always kept in the corner for lessons and took a partial swing, careful not to hit the carpet.

"Why did you stop your swing?" he asked.

"I didn't want to tear the carpet, Harvey."

"Don't take a swing at all," he told me, "unless you're going to sweep a spot."

I didn't want to take a chance, but he insisted, so I did it, finishing my swing—fortunately—without ripping a divot out of his carpet. At ninety, he still practiced the tenets of golf that he believed in so strongly, even in his living room. Finish that swing. Always. Even in practice.

Q: I'm not very good. How do I play with more experienced golfers?

A: As long as you keep up, you'll always be able to find a game. Suppose we were waiting on the first tee and two players approached and one said, "I shoot even par," and the other said, "I play fast." The fast player will be extended the first invitation.

Actually, many of the problems that plague golf today were unwittingly created by the golf industry. I'll give you two examples: slow play, the number one problem in golf, and tension, the number one problem in golf swings.

Are golfers ever told how many practice swings to take? Are they ever told how long to stand over the ball before hitting it?

No, they're not. How, then, could new golfers be expected to know? No one's ever given them any direction. While it's outside the scope of this book to go into detail about the social rules that govern the game, there is a book that comes to mind. Recommended by Messrs. Penick, Kite, and Crenshaw, it's entitled *Golf Etiquette,* written by Puett and Apfelbaum.

One other point about speed of play: Players often have to be reminded to pay attention to the group in front of them, and to forget about the group behind. As long as you're keeping pace with the preceding group, you're fulfilling your obligation.

Limiting practice swings and recognizing that the longer we stand over the ball, the more tension we build, will help us play better golf.

Q: How can I stay positive when I'm playing poorly?

A: We've periodically touched on ways of dealing with pressure and the detrimental effects of being overly critical. I'll never forget that after a round, Harvey would say, "Tell me about your good shots." When I tried to move on to the gory details, to the fiery derailments and the intrinsic unfairness of golf, he'd shake his head and repeat, "No, the good ones."

I used to kid him that he just wanted to hear shorter stories, but as an instructor, I see his point. Harvey certainly understood that the longer the whining continues, the longer it takes us to get on with it.

Tom Kite certainly took the lesson to heart. I've never heard him complain about his putting or ball striking, or any fleeting aspect of his game. Whether he was on top, as golf's all-time money winner, or mired in a slump, in response to a question about his play, he'd always reply, "it's getting better." Harvey counselled competitive players to surround themselves with positive, upbeat people, not complainers. If your game is going sour, let it go. Focus on improving, on the future, not the past. Tell me about your good shots.

Why dwell on the last shot? It's gone. There's the old saying: The most important shot in golf is the next one, the one you're preparing to hit. Concentrate on what needs to be done on this shot instead of trying to figure out what you did wrong on the last one. Stay in the present.

Q: *I'm interested in golf but I'm not into being competitive. How should I approach it?*

A: It's amazing how frequently taking the game "seriously" comes up. It reminds me of playing with three friends that I hadn't seen for several months. We had some catching up to do. On the fourth hole we each hit our drives and couldn't find Marilyn's. After a few minutes I turned to her and asked where she thought it was. She couldn't remember. The four of us finally looked at each other and realized we hadn't found it because she'd never hit it! We were so engrossed in visiting, after the three of us had hit, we jumped in our carts and took off down the fairway.

Something does need to be said about respecting a playing partner's seriousness about her game. In the above story, if one of us had been trying to play well instead of talking, the other three would have done the same thing. There are varying degrees of social golf, and it pays to be aware of the differences.

Another suggestion is to not feel obligated to keep score. Take pleasure in hitting good shots and don't feel locked in to playing 18 holes. Play nine, or play by yourself until you feel more comfortable.

Q: How do I get involved in networking with golf?

A: Business golf, client development, whatever the latest euphemism is, mixing golf and business is about relationships. Deals may not necessarily, if ever, be cut on the golf course; but given the choice between a round of golf and a cold call or a four-hour meeting, which would you chose? Is it any wonder that golf and business have become so cozy, so much so that a commentator notes that corporate giving is now on the *Golf Standard?*

Charity has provided corporate America with a truly win-win situation. Those looking to make contacts, to meet power brokers in their industry and community, gather in a nonthreatening and healthful environment. The charity walks out a winner at the end of the day. So does the community, and everyone can feel good about making a contribution. Taking the additional step of sponsorship, as so many leading companies have, is worth an unlimited amount of goodwill and contacts.

To succeed in business golf, one need only have appropriate equipment, know golf etiquette, and have a cursory knowledge of professional golf (it's on TV just about every weekend). Beyond that, by simply asking someone about their game, or helping them find their ball, the sky's the limit. Doors will open, and making friends as well as contacts is entirely possible. Indicative of the importance of golf, students now tell me that their companies frequently pick up the cost of their golf lessons. And for several years, I've taught golf classes of female MBA students at the University of Texas.

The prevalence of golf in company retreats, outings, and conferences is just one more compelling reason, if any were needed, for giving the game a try. Golf's increasing popularity should hardly come as a surprise. It is the one game that everyone can play, which players of different skills can compete and enjoy together.

The learning of golf is a slow and tedious process at the best; though illumined by many bright flashes of hope, the clouds of despair darken it at least in equal number. The exasperating thing is that the secret seems always to be escaping you; for a day, perhaps for a week, you may surprise and delight yourself by playing your iron to the general admiration. You think you have acquired the stroke of beauty as a joy for ever: the next day it may have utterly gone from you. The consolation is that it will return. . . . It seems that she [golf] will never yield up all her secrets. "Age cannot wither, nor custom stale her infinite variety."

—Horace Hutchinson,
"A Gossip on Golf," 1896

Index